Jouvenalliss M.K,

Po box 1482 00200,

Nairobi,Kenya.

Email:jouvenalliss@gmail.com

FALL TO FLY

Jouvenalliss .M.K.

Table of contents

Avowal

First of all, my greatest gratitude goes to the Almighty God. His Grace has been sufficient. To my dad and mum, Benedict and Victoria for their Heroic Parenting. My brothers and Sisters for always being there for me. The many leaders who inspired me in different ways. My lovely Boys Brummelhuis and Beelbright for the concerted effort they accorded to me during the long hours of drafting and writing this book. And finally, to my lovely wife Zemenay who has been a central pillar in my life. A confidant who always inspired me to write, write and write. Thank you all may God bless you.

Foreword

In the vast tapestry of human existence, success often emerges as an elusive beacon, surrounded by the shadows of doubt, fear, and failure. We are taught to fear the fall, to avoid missteps, and to view failure as the ultimate defeat. But what if failure itself held the key to our most extraordinary achievements? What if the very notion we perceive as our downfall could become the catalyst for our greatest rise?

Jouvenalliss Mwendwa Kioko stands as a beacon of hope, resilience, and unwavering determination. Through his multifaceted roles as a man of God, life coach, mentor, and writer, he continues to inspire individuals from all walks of life to over-come adversity and achieve greatness.

In this guide, he embarks on a transformative journey of self-discovery and empowerment. Welcome to "Fall to Fly," a motivational guide that challenges the conventional belief that failure is an endpoint, revealing instead its hidden potential as a stepping stone towards greatness. Within these chapters, Jouvenalliss shatters the shackles of self-doubt and embrace the significance of failure and adversity as the forge that shapes our character and propels us towards our desired destinations. Drawing inspiration from remarkable individuals throughout history who faced adversity head-on, he unveil strategic moves and essential steps that ignite the fire within, leading us to our own extraordinary success.

He quotes Amelia Earhart, the daring aviator who defied societal norms and soared through the skies which reminds us of the transformative power of risk-taking. Through her audacity and relentless pursuit of her dreams, she shattered barriers and left an indelible mark on the world. Her story will inspire us to conquer our fears and take bold leaps towards our destined motion.

Alongside Amelia, jouvenallis quotes the exact words of Charles Lindbergh, the pioneer aviator who epitomized the spirit of calculated risk-taking. His words will echo in our minds, challenging us to break free from the confines of fear and embrace chances that push the boundaries of what we thought possible. Through his guidance, we will learn that a life devoid of daring is but a half-lived existence. But "Fall to Fly" is more than a mere collection of stories and wisdom from extraordinary individuals. It is a beacon of hope, a roadmap for transforming failures into stepping stones towards a brighter future. It offers invaluable insights and practical tools to reshape our mindset, overcome obstacles, and unleash the hidden potential that lies dormant within each of us.

Whether you seek personal or professional growth, "Fall to Fly" will serve as your guide to navigate the turbulent waters of life, transforming failures into fuel for success. It is an empowering testament to the resilience of the human spirit, a reminder that within each of us lies a giant waiting to be awakened. So, dear reader, let us embark together on this remarkable journey of self-discovery. Open your heart and mind, for the secrets of success and the magics of failure await. Get ready to embrace failure, take risks, and soar to new heights. Let us dare to fall, so we may truly learn to fly.

***

Foreword by:

Beverly Sharma.

Renown motivational speaker,

Founder & C.E.O: Sharma Consultants.

Prologue

Failure is known to many as lack of success and defeat. But to me, failure is the key to success. The starting point of new ventures. The opportunity to reach great heights, and to learn more from your mistakes. It is the bridge that helps you to cross the river of sadness, worry, and rejection. The only way when failure can be termed as lack of success is when you realize your failure and do nothing about it. For you to achieve success, failure is a paramount and an essential facet of your path. Learn how to appreciate mistakes but most importantly learn a lesson from each and every mistake you commit. Learn to embrace challenges and each challenge you come across, make it a bridge to your next level. No one has ever reached the top of a mountain without climbing the mountain. For you to climb a mountain, you must also start from the ground and that is where you start encountering the challenges hence learning how to cope up with them.

In this guide, the captivating stories of individuals who reached acmes of success during adversity are given in a simple language with an aim of encouraging and inspiring many people who usually view failure as the end of their life.

"Fall to Fly" emphasizes several key elements that contribute to the magic of success:

1. Embracing Failure:

The book highlights the significance of failure as a catalyst for personal growth. It encourages readers to view failure not as the ultimate defeat, but as a stepping stone towards success. By embracing failure, individuals can learn valuable lessons, adapt their strategies, and develop resilience to overcome future challenges.

2. Learning from Adversity:

The book recognizes that adversity is an inevitable part of life's journey. It encourages readers to see obstacles as opportunities for growth and self-improvement. By learning from adversity, individuals can develop new skills, gain wisdom, and strengthen their character, enabling them to navigate future challenges with greater ease.

3. Taking Calculated Risks:

The book draws inspiration from figures like Amelia Earhart, who took audacious risks to achieve greatness. It emphasizes the importance of calculated risk-taking, where individuals carefully assess the potential rewards and consequences before making bold moves. By stepping out of their comfort zones and taking strategic risks, individuals can open doors to new opportunities and expand their horizons.

4. Reshaping Mindset:

"Fall to Fly" recognizes the power of mindset in achieving success. It encourages readers to cultivate a positive and growth-oriented mindset, where failures are viewed as temporary setbacks rather than permanent defeats. By reframing their thoughts and beliefs, individuals can develop a resilient and optimistic attitude, enabling them to overcome challenges and stay focused on their goals.

5. Unleashing Inner Potential:

The book emphasizes that success lies within each individual. It guides readers to tap into their unique strengths, talents, and passions to unlock their true potential. By embracing self-discovery and recognizing their innate abilities, individuals can align their goals with their authentic selves, leading to a sense of fulfillment and accomplishment.

Continuous Learning and Growth: "Fall to Fly" underscores the importance of continuous learning and personal development. It encourages readers to seek knowledge, acquire new skills, and stay adaptable in a rapidly changing world. By embracing a growth mindset and consistently expanding their knowledge and abilities, individuals can stay ahead of the curve and seize opportunities for success.

In summary, the magic of success, as depicted in "Fall to Fly," lies in embracing failure, learning from adversity, taking calculated risks, reshaping mindset, unleashing inner potential, and pursuing continuous growth. By incorporating these elements into their lives, individuals can transform setbacks into stepping stones, overcome challenges, and embark on a remarkable journey of personal and professional success.

AXIOMS OF SUCCESS

Embracing failure

Embracing failure without being hurt involves adopting a positive mindset and implementing strategies that help you learn and grow from your setbacks. Here are some steps to embrace failure effectively:

1. Reframe Failure:

Instead of viewing failure as a negative outcome, reframe it as a valuable learning experience. Recognize that failure is a natural part of any journey towards success and an opportunity for growth. See it as a stepping stone on the path to achieving your goals.

2. Separate Failure from Self-Worth:

Understand that failure does not define your worth as an individual. Your value as a person is not tied to your failures or successes. By separating your self-worth from the outcome of a specific endeavor, you can avoid taking failure personally and maintain a healthy perspective.

3. Analyze and Learn:

Take time to analyze your failures objectively. Identify the factors that led to the setback, evaluate your decisions and actions, and extract valuable lessons from the experience. By understanding what went wrong and why, you can adjust your approach and make improvements for future endeavors.

4. Practice Self-Compassion:

Be kind to yourself and practice self-compassion when facing failure. Treat yourself with understanding and empathy, just as you would support a friend or loved one who experienced a setback. Remember that everyone makes mistakes, and failure is an opportunity for growth, not a reflection of your abilities or character.

5. Set Realistic Expectations:

Avoid setting unrealistic expectations for yourself. Understand that failure is a possibility, even when you give your best effort. Set achievable goals and be prepared for the potential obstacles and setbacks that may arise along the way. This will help you approach failure with resilience and a proactive mindset.

6. Seek Support:

Surround yourself with a supportive network of family, friends, or mentors who can offer guidance and encouragement during challenging times. Sharing your experiences and seeking advice from others who have overcome failure can provide valuable insights and emotional support.

7. Take Action and Persist:

After learning from your failures, take the lessons you've gained and apply them to your future endeavors. Use failure as motivation to persist and keep moving forward. By maintaining a growth mindset and using failure as a stepping stone, you can increase your chances of eventual success.

Remember, embracing failure is not about avoiding pain entirely but rather about transforming setbacks into valuable learning experiences. By cultivating resilience, self-compassion, and a growth mindset, you can navigate failure with a sense of empowerment and emerge stronger on the path to achieving your goals.

Axioms of success 1

1. Embracing failure

Extraordinary you

Being extraordinary in a world that may consider you a failure requires a shift in perspective and a determination to rise above external judgments. Here are the leads to cultivate extraordinariness in the face of perceived failure:

1. Redefine your Destiny:

Challenge conventional definitions of destiny and create your own metrics for what it means to be extraordinary. Instead of solely focusing on external achievements or societal expectations, consider qualities like personal growth, resilience, authenticity, and making a positive impact on others' lives. By aligning your definition of destiny with your values, you can find fulfillment and purpose, regardless of external judgment.

2. Embrace Your Uniqueness:

Embrace your individuality and recognize that what sets you apart can be a source of strength and innovation. Celebrate your unique talents, perspectives, and experiences. Rather than trying to fit into preconceived notions of success, channel your energy into expressing your authentic self and leveraging your distinct qualities to make a difference.

3. Cultivate a Growth Mindset:

Adopt a growth mindset, which is the belief that abilities and intelligence can be developed through effort and learning. Embrace challenges as opportunities for growth, view failures as valuable feedback, and persist in the face of setbacks. See each experience, even the ones labeled as failures, as a chance to learn, improve, and evolve.

4. Focus on Continuous Learning:

Dedicate yourself to lifelong learning and personal development. Acquire new skills, seek knowledge, and stay curious. By expanding your knowledge base and acquiring diverse perspectives, you can bring fresh insights and innovative solutions to your endeavors, setting yourself apart from the norm.

5. Find Your Passion and Purpose:

Discover and pursue your true passions and align them with a sense of purpose. When you engage in activities that genuinely inspire and motivate you, your dedication and enthusiasm will shine through. By pursuing what truly

lights a fire within you, you can create extraordinary outcomes that transcend societal expectations.

6. Surround Yourself with Support- ive Networks:

Surround yourself with individuals who support and believe in your potential, rather than
those who reinforce negative judgments. Seek
out mentors, coaches, or communities that
share your values and provide encouragement,
guidance, and constructive feedback. Collabo-
rate with like-minded individuals who can help
you grow and expand your horizons.

7. Lead by Example:

Be a role model for others by embodying qualities of resilience, authenticity, and unwavering

determination. Share your journey openly, including both successes and setbacks, to inspire and empower others to embrace their own extraordinariness. By leading with integrity and authenticity, you can inspire positive change and challenge societal perceptions of failure.

Remember, being extraordinary is not about conforming to societal norms or meeting external expectations. It is about embracing your unique qualities, pursuing your passions, and making a meaningful impact on your terms. By redefining success, cultivating a growth mindset, continuous learning, and surrounding yourself with support, you can transcend perceived failure and create a life that is truly extraordinary.

Axioms of success 2

1. **Embracing failure**
2. **Extraordinary you.**

Awaken the giant

Awakening the giant within is a lifelong journey. It requires self-reflection, continuous growth, a positive mindset, and taking intentional action. Embrace your unique qualities, believe in your potential, and fearlessly pursue your dreams. By tapping into your inner giant, you can unleash your full potential and create a life of purpose, fulfillment, and extraordinary achievement.

To awaken the giant within you, here are the essential steps to take:

1. Self-Reflection and Awareness:

Take time for self-reflection to gain a deeper understanding of your strengths, passions, values, and aspirations. Engage in practices like journaling, meditation, or mindfulness to develop self-awareness. Recognize your potential and believe in your ability to make a significant impact in the world.

2. Self-Reflection and Awareness:

Set clear and inspiring goals that align with your passions and values. Make them challenging yet attainable, and break them down into smaller, actionable steps. Goals provide direction, focus, and motivation, and they allow you to tap into your inner potential to achieve extraordinary results.

3. Continuous Learning and Personal Growth:

Commit to lifelong learning and personal growth. Expand your knowledge, acquire new skills, and challenge yourself to step out of your comfort zone. Seek opportunities to develop and refine your talents, whether through formal education, workshops, online courses, or mentorship programs. Embrace feedback and view failures as opportunities for growth.

4. Positive Mindset and Self-Belief:

Cultivate a positive mindset and develop a strong belief in yourself and your abilities. Challenge self-limiting beliefs and replace them with empowering thoughts. Surround yourself with positive influences, affirmations, and supportive people who uplift and inspire you. Focus on your strengths and past achievements to boost your confidence.

5. Take Action and Embrace Challenges:

Take bold action towards your goals and embrace challenges as opportunities for growth
and learning. Step outside your comfort zone
and embrace calculated risks. Accept that failure and setbacks are part of the journey and
view them as valuable lessons. Stay resilient
and persevere through obstacles, knowing that
each experience brings you closer to your full
potential.

6. Cultivate a Growth Mindset:

Adopt a growth mindset, believing that your
abilities and intelligence can be developed
through effort, practice, and learning. Embrace
challenges, seek feedback, and persist in the
face of setbacks. See failures as temporary

setbacks and opportunities for growth, rather than as indications of fixed limitations.

7. Practice Self-Care and Well-being:

Take care of your physical, mental, and emotional well-being. Prioritize self-care activities like exercise, proper nutrition, restful sleep, and stress management. Nurture healthy relationships and surround yourself with a supportive network. When you take care of yourself, you have the energy and resilience to tap into your full potential.

8. Serve Others and Make a Difference:

Find ways to contribute to the well-being of others and make a positive impact. Use your unique skills, talents, and resources to help others and create positive change in your community or beyond. When you serve others, you not only awaken the giant within yourself, but you also inspire and uplift others to do the same.

Axioms of success 3

1. **Embracing failure**
2. **Extraordinary you.**
3. **Awaken the giant in you**

Embrace Networking

Success in networking is crucial for building relationships, creating opportunities, and achieving personal and professional growth. Here are some key strategies to help you succeed in networking:

1. Define Your Networking Goals:

Clarify your networking objectives. Are you seeking career opportunities, business partnerships, knowledge exchange, or personal development? Having clear goals will guide your networking efforts and help you focus on the right connections.

2. Build Genuine Relationships:

Approach networking with a genuine desire to connect and build meaningful relationships. Show interest in others, actively listen, and engage in authentic conversations. Be approachable, friendly, and empathetic. Look for ways to provide value and support to others without expecting immediate returns.

3. Attend Networking Events:

Attend industry conferences, seminars, workshops, and community events relevant to your interests or field. These gatherings provide excellent opportunities to meet like-minded individuals, experts, and potential mentors. Be prepared with a concise introduction and thoughtful questions to initiate conversations.

4. Utilize Online Platforms:

Leverage online platforms like LinkedIn, professional forums, and social media to expand your network. Join relevant groups, participate in discussions, and share valuable content. Actively engage with others by commenting on their posts and connecting with individuals who align with your goals.

5. Follow Up and Nurture Relationships:

After meeting new contacts, follow up with personalized messages or emails to express your appreciation for the conversation and to continue the connection. Stay in touch regularly by sharing relevant articles, insights, or opportunities. Offer support when needed, and celebrate others' successes.

6. Provide Value to Others:

Networking is a two-way street. Look for opportunities to help and support others in your network. Share your expertise, offer resources or introductions, and be a connector. Being known as a reliable and helpful person will strengthen your relationships and increase the likelihood of reciprocity.

7. Attend Networking Groups or Associations:

Join industry-specific networking groups, professional associations, or alumni networks. Engage actively by attending meetings, participating in committees, and volunteering for leadership roles. These groups provide access to a targeted network and offer opportunities for deeper connections.

8. Be Authentic and Memorable:

Showcase your unique qualities and strengths in networking situations. Be confident in expressing your passions and aspirations. Craft a compelling personal story that communicates your values, experiences, and goals. Leave a positive and memorable impression by being authentic and memorable.

9. Maintain an Online Presence:

Cultivate an online presence that showcases your expertise and interests. Create a professional profile on platforms like LinkedIn and maintain an up-to-date and compelling online presence. Share your insights, achievements, and experiences to establish credibility and attract opportunities

Remember, successful networking requires consistent effort, patience, and a genuine interest in building relationships. Focus on giving rather than solely seeking to receive. By nurturing authentic connections, providing value, and leveraging opportunities, you can expand your network, unlock new possibilities, and achieve personal and professional success.

Axioms of success 4

1. **Embracing failure**

2. **Extraordinary you.**

3. **Awaken the giant in you.**

4. **Embrace networking**

Success in the face of adversity:

Success is not only achieved when things are leading to one another. The following examples demonstrate that success can be achieved even in the face of immense adversity. These individuals not only overcame their challenges but also made substantial contributions to their respective fields, leaving a lasting impact on the world. Their stories inspire us to persevere, pursue our dreams, and turn adversity into an opportunity for growth and achievement.

1. Nelson Mandela:

Nelson Mandela, the former President of South Africa and anti-apartheid activist, spent 27 years in prison for his political beliefs. Despite the immense adversity he faced, Mandela emerged as a symbol of resilience, forgiveness, and reconciliation. After his release, he played a pivotal role in dismantling apartheid and became the first black President of South Africa.

2. Oprah Winfrey:

Oprah Winfrey, a renowned media mogul, talk show host, and philanthropist, faced numerous challenges throughout her life. She experienced a difficult childhood marked by poverty and abuse. However, she overcame those adversities, became a successful television personality, and built a media empire with her own production company, The Oprah Winfrey Network (OWN).

3. Stephen Hawking:

Stephen Hawking, a renowned physicist and cosmologist, was diagnosed with amyotrophic lateral sclerosis (ALS) at the age of 21. Despite the progressive nature of the disease and being wheelchair-bound, Hawking made significant contributions to the field of theoretical physics and became one of the most brilliant scientific minds of our time.

4. Malala Yousafzai:

Malala Yousafzai, a Pakistani activist and Nobel laureate, faced adversity as she advocated for girls' education in the Swat Valley, where the Taliban had banned girls from attending school. At the age of 15, she survived an assassination attempt by the Taliban, which only strengthened her resolve. Malala continues to fight for girls' education globally and has become an influential voice for change.

5. Vincent Van Gogh:

Vincent Van Gogh, the Dutch post-impressionist painter, faced significant mental health challenges throughout his life. He struggled with depression, anxiety, and self-doubt. Despite his inner turmoil, Van Gogh created over 2,000 artworks, including iconic paintings like "Starry

Night" and "Sunflowers." Today, he is celebrated as one of the most influential artists in
history.

Axioms of success 5

1. **Embracing failure**

2. **Extraordinary you.**

3. **Awaken the giant in you.**

4. **Embrace networking**

5. **Success in the face of adversity**

Focus beyond failure

When everything seems doomed and you feel like you're at a low point, it can be challenging to find the strength to rise. However, here are some techniques you can use to help lift yourself up:

1. Acceptance and Self-Compassion:

Start by accepting the current situation and acknowledging your emotions. Allow yourself to feel what you're experiencing without judgment. Practice self-compassion by treating yourself with kindness and understanding. Remind yourself that setbacks and challenges are a part of life, and it's okay to struggle.

2. Reframe Your Perspective:

Challenge negative thoughts and reframe your perspective. Instead of dwelling on what is going wrong, focus on what you can learn from the situation and how it can contribute to your personal growth. Look for silver linings or opportunities for change and improvement. Adopt a mindset of resilience and see setbacks as temporary hurdles on your journey.

3. Set Small, Achievable Goals:

Break down your larger goals into smaller, manageable tasks. Setting achievable goals provides a sense of direction and accomplishment. Celebrate even the smallest victories along the way to maintain motivation and build momentum. Each step forward, no matter how small, contributes to progress and a sense of empowerment.

4. Seek Support and Connection:

Reach out to trusted friends, family members, or mentors who can provide emotional support and guidance. Share your struggles and concerns with them, and don't hesitate to ask for help when needed. Connecting with others who have faced similar challenges can also provide valuable insights and encouragement.

5. Practice Self-Care:

Prioritize self-care activities that nourish your physical, mental, and emotional well-being. Engage in activities that bring you joy, such as exercise, hobbies, spending time in nature, or engaging in creative pursuits. Take care of your physical health by eating nutritious meals, getting enough sleep, and practicing relaxation techniques like deep breathing or meditation.

6. Seek Inspiration:

Surround yourself with positive and inspiring influences. Read books, watch movies, or listen to podcasts that uplift and motivate you. Seek out stories of individuals who have overcome adversity and achieved success. Draw inspiration from their journeys and use their experiences as a reminder that you too can overcome your challenges.

7. Focus on Gratitude:

Practice gratitude by reflecting on the things you are grateful for, even in difficult times. Cultivating a gratitude mindset helps shift your focus towards the positive aspects of your life and fosters resilience. Consider keeping a gratitude journal, where you write down three things you are grateful for each day.

8. Take Action and Persist:

Take small steps towards your goals, even if they seem insignificant at first. Taking action creates momentum and helps you regain a sense of control. Persevere through challenges, setbacks, and failures. Remember that setbacks are not permanent unless you give up. Stay determined and keep moving forward, adapting your strategies as necessary.

Remember, raising yourself up when everything seems doomed takes time and effort. Be patient with yourself and celebrate your progress along the way. By employing these techniques, you can gradually regain your con-fidence, find new possibilities, and start build-ing a brighter future

Axioms of success 6

1. **Embracing failure**
2. **Extraordinary you.**
3. **Awaken the giant in you.**
4. **Embrace networking**
5. **Success in the face of adversity**
6. **Focus beyond your failure**

Redefine success

I didn't get the real meaning of success for many years. In many ways and from many sources. I have searched in all corners of the world. I have interacted with a good many of people from all walks of life. I have inquired and discussed with everyone I have ever met about the meaning of success but; Almost everyone thinks success is having a lot of money, property, and being so much educated. Holding a very senior position in the society and commanding a big chain of achievement in terms of finance and property.

The Oxford dictionary defines success as the fact that you have achieved what you want; doing well and becoming famous, and rich among other things. If you ask a small child what success is, the child will tell you it's being able to buy candy and other lovely things by himself. If you ask a beggar what success is, he will tell you it's having money and having not to beg again. If you ask a jobless person, what success is he will tell you it's securing a job. If you ask a rich person, what success is he will tell you it's owning the whole world. All these are different views of success. But to me, this is where I find success.

"Laughing often and much every day;
And winning the recognition and respect of the wise;
And the love of young ones.
To be criticized for the obvious,
And accepting with pure heart those who betray you in disguise.
Finding the best in everyone you meet, and appreciating beauty as it is.
To live the world more comfortably;
Be it through a healthy start, a harvest patch,
Or an elevated living condition, But most importantly,
To know that even one face has smiled,
Because of your effort.

:M.K Jouvenalliss from Oomph bells
***

The big five of success
(Dream)

If you mention the lion, the elephant, the leopard, the buffalo, and the rhino, what lingers in the mind of everyone is the big five of the jungle. They rule over all the other animals in the forest and they control them at all times. They dictate what happens in the forest. And that's what makes them the big 5. Likewise, every person who wants to succeed in life must have a dream. A dream with a deadline. The big five of success. Below are the cardinal big five. They dictate what happens in the realm of success and prosperity. They also set the close-grained foundation of growth and augmentation:

D-Determination

R-Relationship

E-Excellency

A-Action

M-Management

Let's look at each one of them individually.

Determination

This is the quality of having firmly decided to do something even though it seems difficult. Zacchaeus was a very short man and he was stressed to see who Jesus was. But he could not make to see Jesus because of the crowd which had followed the Messiah. So, he climbed up on a sycamore tree to be able to see Jesus. Because of his determination,

Zacchaeus saw Jesus, ate and drank with him in his house.

Today many people fail because they are not determined to achieve what they want in their lives. If they encounter a challenge, they usually back down allowing themselves to be defeated.

Focus ahead, walk the walk, and talk the talk. Stick to the decision and hold on to your principles. Pray too and trust in God because he has promised to pave a way for his people.

"I will make a highway across the mountains and prepare a road for my people to travel" ISAIAH 49:11.

Even if the situation you want to pursue is as big as a mountain, just believe that you will make it. Ralph Waldo Emerson once said; *"Difficulties exist to be surmounted."*

Relationship

This is the way people, groups, and nations among other things feel about or behave towards each other. It is the ability to get along with others.

Relationships between human beings are the most fascinating bearing in mind that man is nature's greatest miracle. As many as we are, Billions and billions of us throughout the world, none resembles the other. In character, size and appearance.

Everyone is special in their ways, so God values all of us. As weak as we are to him, his thoughts to us are as good as the work he did; Creating us.

The law of gratitude puts it clear; *that the more you appreciate what you have, the more life throws you away.* The only way we can show gratitude is by making the best out of what we have. Possessing the image and like-ness of God is such a great privilege and more so a blessing. It will be such an ingratitude if you don't make the most of your opportunity by getting along with everyone, regardless of their tribe, religion, colour, race, nationality, and even position in society. Many people lose because they don't know how to socialize with others while others gain just because of having a smile on their face and being good to others.

Once, a young man achieved an impressive feat by graduating with first-class honors from a renowned university. His academic success attracted the attention of several esteemed companies, all eager to hire him with lucrative salaries. Among the offers he received, he carefully selected the most promising oppor-tunity, turning down the rest with unwavering confidence in his exceptional qualifications. With great anticipation, he prepared himself meticulously for the upcoming interview.

On the day of the interview, the young man donned a stylish, brand-new Black Hoffner suit paired with sleek black Russini shoes. His outfit was complemented by a crisp white shirt, a charming red polka dot tie, and a pocket square. He added a touch of elegance with a dazzling golden lapel pin and tie pin. Undeniably, he exuded an air of sophistication and readiness for the job. Filled with hope, he boarded a matatu, the local transportation, heading towards the premises of the esteemed company.

During the journey, as the matatu made its usual stops to pick up passengers, a middle-aged man, dressed in a worn-out suit and black shoes, boarded the vehicle. He secured a seat next to the young graduate, unintentionally stepping on the young man's immaculate shoe. The young graduate was deeply upset by this incident. The remorseful older gentleman promptly apologized, sincerely regretting his mistake. However, to the young man's disappointment, he refused to accept the apology, allowing his anger to surface.

Fueled by frustration, the young graduate raised his voice towards the older man, demanding to know why he hadn't recognized his impeccable appearance. "What's wrong with you? Can't you see how well-dressed I am?" he exclaimed. The older man, with utmost politeness, expressed his remorse once more, pleading for forgiveness. The young man harshly dismissed his plea, exclaiming, "Apologies won't restore the shine to my shoes! You should learn to respect the status of others!"

Despite the young man's heated words, the older man remained silent, listening patiently to the barrage of criticism. They both disembarked at the same stop, and the older man, leading by example, stepped off the matatu first. As he turned back to the young graduate, he humbly requested forgiveness once more, saying, "Please find it in your heart to forgive me, my son."

However, the young graduate paid no attention to his plea. Instead, he busied himself with brushing off the damage to his shoes. The older man, deeply affected by the youngster's callous attitude, left, carrying the weight of this encounter with him.

The young man proceeded to the company where he had been invited for an interview. As he arrived, he noticed several other candidates awaiting their turn. His name was called, making him the third to enter the interview room. But as he stepped through the door, he was engulfed by the greatest shock of his life. The only person seated there, the sole determiner of his fate, was the very same older man he had encountered on the matatu. It was the man he had insulted, belittled, and disregarded when he had offered his sincere apology.

Confusion and distress overwhelmed the young man. He desperately wanted to apologize, but his voice failed him. Searching for an escape, he glanced around the room, feeling the weight of his misjudgment. Seated in the interview chair without an invitation, he tearfully expressed his realization to the old man, confessing his ignorance of their imminent reunion. Regrettably, it was too late to rectify his mistake.

"You possess the qualities we seek in this role, Mr. Denzel," the old man stated with a hint of sorrow. "However, I am sorry to say that you have already failed the interview," the old man concluded, his words piercing through Denzel's heart. Denzel, overcome with a mix of emotions, left the office with a sullen expression on his face. Confusion and despair washed over him as he reflected on the opportunity he had lost due to his rude, mean-spirited, and disrespectful attitude towards a fellow citizen.

As Denzel walked away, the weight of his actions sank in. He realized the profound impact that his behavior had on the course of events. It was a hard lesson to learn, but one that would forever stay with him. Regret flooded his thoughts, and he couldn't help but imagine how different things could have been if only he had chosen kindness and understanding over anger and entitlement.

Days turned into weeks, and Denzel found himself at a crossroad. The rejection from that pivotal interview haunted him, serving as a constant reminder of the importance of empathy and respect. Determined to grow from his past mistakes, he embarked on a journey of self-reflection and personal development.

Denzel recognized that true success went beyond academic achievements and material appearances. It encompassed qualities such as humility, compassion, and the ability to treat others with kindness. With this newfound understanding, he actively sought opportunities to volunteer and engage with people from diverse backgrounds, listening to their stories and learning from their experiences.

Months passed, and Denzel's transformation became evident. He became known for his genuine empathy, unwavering respect, and willingness to lend a helping hand. As he immersed himself in various community projects, he discovered the joy of making a positive impact on others' lives, finding fulfillment in selfless acts of kindness.

One fateful day, as Denzel walked through the bustling city streets, he noticed a familiar face in the crowd. It was the old man from the matatu—the very person he had treated with disdain and caused such regrettable consequences. Filled with both trepidation and hope, Denzel approached him, mustering the courage to offer a sincere apology.

With a mixture of surprise and forgiveness, the old man smiled warmly at Denzel. "My son, I have long since forgiven you," he said, his voice gentle and filled with understanding. "I saw the change within you, witnessed your growth, and I am proud of the person you have become."

Touched by the old man's generosity of spirit, Denzel felt a renewed sense of purpose. He understood that the greatest redemption lay not in the forgiveness of others but in the transformation of oneself. The encounter served as a constant reminder of the importance of treating everyone with dignity and respect, regardless of their appearance or social standing.

Armed with a humbled heart and a newfound appreciation for the value of empathy, Denzel's journey continued. He pursued his professional aspirations with renewed determination, always mindful of the lessons he had learned. And as he moved forward, he made it his mission to inspire others to embrace kindness, compassion, and the understanding that true success encompassed not only personal achievements but also the positive impact we have on those around us.

In time, Denzel's journey led him to new opportunities, where he thrived not only professionally but also as a compassionate and respected member of society. His story became a testament to the power of personal growth, forgiveness, and the profound impact our actions can have on others.

And so, Denzel's life unfolded, forever shaped by the lessons he learned that fateful day on the matatu.

Excellency

To truly reach the pinnacle of success, one must strive for excellence in every endeavor, no matter how big or small, casual or professional. It is crucial to imbue each action with significance, irrespective of whether it is perceived as important by others. This dedication and attention to detail become the defining characteristic of success.

Consider a skilled chef employed at a prestigious 5-star hotel in Asia, renowned for his mastery in preparing Biryani rice. Every morning, as he arrives at work, he meticulously gathers the necessary ingredients for this delectable dish. Should any ingredient be missing, he steadfastly refuses to proceed. A curious colleague, perplexed by this unwavering commitment, inquires, "Why do you insist on having all the ingredients? Some can be omitted without affecting the final outcome. Besides, the customers are unaware of the cooking process, so why does it truly matter?"

The chef turns to his colleague, gazing earnestly into their eyes, and imparts a profound truth, "It is not about whether it matters to the customers or anyone else. It matters immensely to me because I believe in doing what is right." In this simple yet profound statement, the chef encapsulates the essence of his unwavering dedication to excellence, his refusal to compromise on his principles, and his relentless pursuit of perfection.

Doing what is right and to the best of your knowledge gives you peace of mind and confidence as you focus ahead on pursuing greater things. Doing what is right even when no one sees you. This is Integrity of the highest degree.

Action-Break the law

This is the ability to take a step towards pursuing a certain thing. Its executing a plan and getting things moving. Without action, you will always hover at the brinks of wishing.

In a tale of ten individuals afflicted by the torment of leprosy, their suffering had confined them to isolation, their hopes dashed by the constraints of the law. Within their collective solitude, two among them harbored a daring notion: to break free from their captivity and seek aid from the benevolent king. Unanimously, they agreed upon this audacious plan. Yet, when the time came to embark on their journey, fear gripped the hearts of eight, dissuading them from venturing forth into a society that had shunned them for so long.

Undeterred by the wavering resolve of their companions, the two originators of the plan remained steadfast in their purpose and pro-ceeded according to their design. Astonish-ingly, divine intervention amplified their foot-steps as they made their way towards the king's palace. Inside the palace, amidst a meal shared by the king and his entourage, the reso-nating sound of the approaching steps rever-berated, misleading the monarch into believ-ing an imminent invasion by a formidable army. In a panicked rush, the king and his staff hastily fled the palace, leaving behind a spread of untouched food.

With the palace now theirs to explore, the two courageous individuals partook in the

abandoned feast, gaining strength and suste-
nance. To their astonishment, they also discovered a wealth of resources, which they wisely
employed to secure their treatment, transforming their fortunes in an instant. Tragically,
the remaining eight, paralyzed by their fear of
taking a single step outside their comfort zone,
met their demise, forever lost in their reluc-
tance to embrace risk.

This poignant tale serves as a reminder that in
the face of adversity, it is often those who dare
to defy their apprehensions and pursue their
dreams who are rewarded with unforeseen
opportunities and prosperity.

Fear is a killer, a demon, and a denier. Below is
the real meaning of fear.

- **F**orce
- **E**vidence
- **A**ppearing
- **R**eal

Avoid fear in all ways. It will make you lose golden opportunities. Even in the bible, the first group of people who will never see the kingdom of God are the cowards. *(Revelations 21:8).* Again, a good number of people today fail because they refuse to take a step. Avoiding to take risk for fear of being challenged. Once you take a step, God sees the desire in you, and He fulfils it accordingly.

"I alone know the plan I have for you. Plans to bring you prosperity, and not disaster. Plans to bring about the future you hope for." JEREMIAH 29:11

Management

This is the control or organization of something. Possessing outstanding leadership and managerial qualities are vital for any person who wishes to have success. There are three main areas in which one can cap for a successful management. Be:

(a). A Self-governor

They say that Charity begins at home. There is no way you can manage others if you are unable to manage yourself. Being smart in dealing with your issues, depicts how perfectly you can handle other roles and responsibilities.

(b). A Time warden

Time is a paramount ingredient in the recipe of management

You can never succeed if you don't know how to get along with time. Keep a diary of all your daily undertakings and stick to it no matter what.

(c). Enterprising

This is the ability to be good at finding ways of doing things. As a leader, you must be able to solve issues arising from the people you are managing.

Strategic fall to fly 1
1. Dream

Failure is not defeat

Many people think that when you fail in some-thing of your desire or anything else, you are done and that is the end of life. On the con-trary view failure as the key that unlocks the firm gate of success and prosperity. Success doesn't come easily. It's always locked but you must find the right key to open success. When you are finding something, you have to try sev-eral ways and places. And at times you will be challenged, confused, and even disappointed. Never give up. This is how you find success.

> Failure is a stepping stone and a bridge to your destiny as long as you don't give up and despair. Any time you fall, make sure you get up.

Embrace failure and see it as a bridge to success. By failing:

- You learn from your mistakes. If you don't learn from your mistakes, you will live as a slave of your failure.
- You experience new challenges and know how to get along with them.
- You restructure your way of thinking and come up with new ideas for success.
- You realize millions of opportunities around you that you would not have bothered with if things were all right.
- You develop faith. Many people tend to forget that there is a God who leads each and everything that we do unless they face challenges.

"Ask the Lord to bless your plans and you will be successful in carrying them out." PROVERBS 16:3

- You realize your real friends. Friends come and go. But real friends stick by you even when everyone else has deserted on you. Your real friends are the average of your success.

In failure, one needs to be strong, Focused, and with a positive attitude towards everything. A story is given about a group of 100 monkeys who went to a racing competition. The target was to get to a dais at the top of a very tall building and be crowned a winner regardless of your position of arrival at the Dias. The instructions were very clear; not to take any advice concerning the journey, eat or drink anything on the way during the race. The only mission was to climb and finish the race. A very big crowd was there to witness the

Page | 73

competition. Every monkey looked strong, charming and ready for the race, except one monkey which seemed to be weak and weary. Everyone predicted that it wouldn't get to even half of the race. When the race commenced, just by the side of the road, very delicious foods were seen and some of the monkeys started eating which led to their disqualification. In the first quarter, 90 of the monkeys were disqualified. Only 10 were left in the race. As they continued with the journey, nay speakers started to discourage them saying that there was a very slippery floor at the rooftop just before reaching the dais and so they would slide, fall down and die. On hearing that, nine of the remaining monkeys quitted from the race leaving one monkey on the same. The one monkey which looked weak and the one that everybody thought won't complete the race. The monkey also faced a lot of discouragement but the more discouragement it got, the more strength it gathered to move on with the journey. None of the nay utterances and discouragements stopped it from the journey. Finally, the monkey got to the dais and was crowned a winner. All the people who were around busted in shouts applauding the monkey. Others went in tears when they looked at how weak the monkey was when the race was starting. Then the monkey was asked by one of the judges, "How did you manage to be the sole winner.? All the other competitors couldn't make it...?" the monkey said, "focus. I focused on the race aiming at the target. My attitude towards the competition was positive. I was determined to win but most importantly I trusted God for my success." The judge asked again. "We have also realized that there were a lot of nay speakers who discouraged everyone on the way. How did you escape them.?"

"I pretended to be deaf. So, I didn't hear what they were saying. Over and above, my past failures have taught me how to cope with new challenges and take risks to achieve what I want. When the going becomes tough, I become tough as well" Uttered the monkey.

At times when you want to do something worthwhile you will face a lot of resistance. You will meet dream killers who will do all they can within their capacity to curb you from achieving what you desire. Avoid such kinds of people and keep your distance. David Yotto said very clearly; that *"the power of an idea is measured by the degree of resistance it attracts."* Be sure that once you start a thing and you get resistance, you are on the right track. So, keep going. Just like the monkey, sometimes you have to turn a deaf ear to what others are saying so as to land at your desired destination.

Persist-stick to guns

Quitting should never be your option. You may experience a thousand falls, but success lies in the next step. James Watt failed a thousand times, but every time he failed, he maneuvered a new way of developing his idea. In the thousand-and-one trial, he made it. James Watt remains the epitome of success after failing unfathomable times.

Today everywhere in the world we use his light bulb. Supposing he quitted, what would we be using for light?

Many people do lose hope and despair in their lives just because they have failed.

One of the most successful presidents in the history of America and the world at large, is Abraham Lincoln. He was born in a one room cabin and faced a lot of challenges in life. This is the rough path that led him to the famous white house;

- In **1816, Abraham Lincoln's** family was vacated from their home and he had to find a job to support them.
- In **1818, Abraham Lincoln's** mother passed on and he was left an orphan
- In **1831, Abraham Lincoln** failed in Business for the first time.
- In **1832, Abraham Lincoln** vied for State Legislation but he lost. In the same year, he lost his job, and he

couldn't make it to law school as he desired.

o In **1833, Abraham Lincoln** was given a soft loan by a friend to start a business, but the year ended with his bankruptcy. For the next close to twenty years, he spent time paying the loan.

o In **1834, Abraham Lincoln** vied for the state Legislation again but this time round he won.

o In **1835, Abraham Lincoln** wanted to get married but His partner died leaving his heart Broken into pieces.

o In **1836, Abraham Lincoln** was bed ridden for six months, very ill and weak due to a nervous breakdown.

o In **1838, Abraham Lincoln** wanted to become speaker of the State Legislature but he lost

- In **1840, Abraham Lincoln** wanted to become an elector but he was defeated too.

- In **1843, Abraham Lincoln** Vied for Congress and was defeated.

- In **1846, Abraham Lincoln** vied for Congress again and this time round he won.

- In **1848, Abraham Lincoln** wanted to be re-elected to congress again but he lost

- In **1849, Abraham Lincoln** wanted to work as a Land officer in his home State but he faced a lot of rejection.

- In **1854, Abraham Lincoln** vied for Senate but he lost.

- In **1856, Abraham Lincoln** garnered less than 100 votes in his party's

National Convention, seeking to be nominated as the vice president.

- In **1858, Abraham Lincoln** vied for the Senate once again and Lost.
- In **1860, Abraham Lincoln** vied to be the president of America and he won with flying colours, becoming one of the most powerful and re-spected Presidents in the history of America and the world at large.

Abraham Lincoln is an icon of success and per-sistence right in Adversity. He never quitted at any given point in time. Even when things were very tough, he held tightly on his goals and objectives.

Don't quit just because things are getting tough and worse. Success is yours. You only need to persist. Many folks today fail because of quitting as a result of wishing for quick fix procedures, forgetting that anything valuable takes time to be created. A palace cannot be completed in four days. A mango tree will not bear fruits in a fortnight and yet a baby cannot walk within six months. And so are our lives. We have to go through a certain evolution which usually concocts us for that beautiful hankered haven.

"No mistakes or failure is as bad as to stop and not try again"   ~JOHN WANAMAKER.

Strategic fall to fly 2

1. **Dream**
2. **Persist**

The fall-to-fly cycle

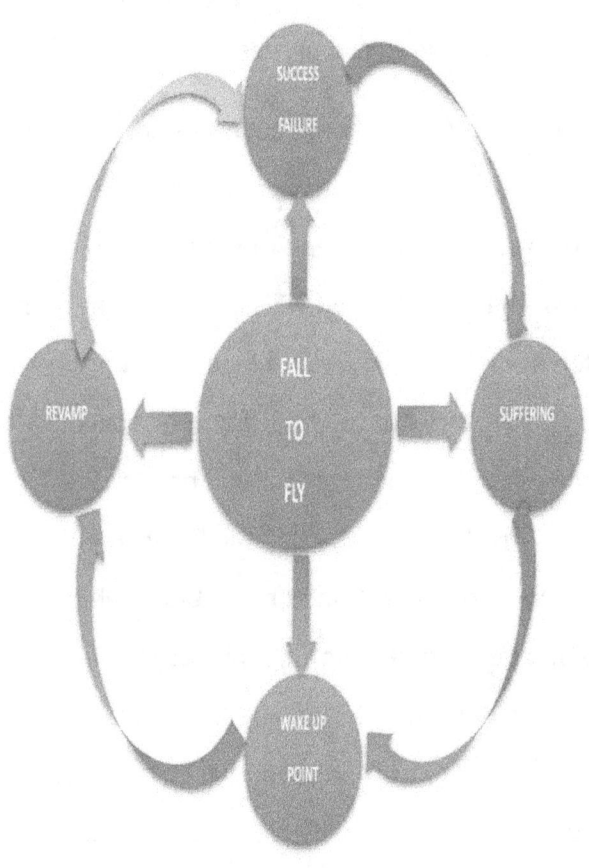

Life is a nature of process, steps, and most importantly a nature of cycles. Fall to Fly is part and parcel of the entire thing of life and we must understand the process.

For you to fail, you must be at the top or have a plan to be there. Perhaps, you have never succeeded at any given time, but you always wish that one day you will come off or be well located. You could be employed and earning a ripping salary but to you that is not a favourable outcome. You feel that you need more than just being on the payroll. Being in either of the above-mentioned ranks brings about resistance of some degree, affliction, hopelessness and at times losing interest in life or anything you are out for. If you fall sick, do you just stay and wait to die.? No. Not at all. You will wake up and pray, get medicine from the pharmacy or even rush to the hospital for treatment.

The same thing applies to our lives. Ups and downs are part and parcel of life. You might pursue a thing over and over again without making it and the question of what could be wrong and why start looming on your mind. Avoid such a question and just remember one thing; failure is part of the process.

"Everything that happens in this world, happens at the right time that God chooses. He sets the time for birth and the time for death. The time for planting and the time for harvesting. The time for killing and the time for healing. The time for tearing down and the time for building. He sets the time for sorrow and the time for joy. The time for mourning and the time for dancing. The time for making love and the time for not making love. The time for kissing and the time for not kissing. He sets the time for finding and the time for losing. The time for saving and the time for throwing away. The time for tearing and the time for mending. The time for silence and the time for talk. He sets the time for love and the time for hate. The time for war and the time for peace."
ECCLESIASTES 3:1-8

So, it's good to know and understand that everything happens with a reason and for a purpose. Ups and downs of this world are part and parcel of the process. There is no way we can live without failing just the same way that there cannot be law without crime, there is no success without failure. And so, we must learn how to appreciate failure as a way of success. But the big question is, what do you do with your failure.? Do you only sit and watch the failure rule over you.? No. You should wake up and focus beyond the failure.

Analyse your Situation

It doesn't matter what kind of challenges you are facing in your current status or in whatever you are pursuing, you only need to analyse your situation and get moving. Consider the following to analyse your situation.

(1). Your origin.

This helps you to understand your circumference. Not merely your surroundings, but simply the ace in hole, which you possess to pursue your desire. Sometimes you could be trying to chase something above your grasp. It is very substantial to be aware of what you can achieve and consequently what you can call upon. For instance, you could be wishing to become the bishop of your church in your fifties and you have never been a pastor throughout your life

(2) Your current position.

Your current status determines what you can easily chase without any physical force, but still achieve your heart's desire. Are you jobless and looking for employment. Working and looking for a greener pasture. Or even do you want to do something else far from being on the payroll. It's good to define what you want since you can't do all things.

(3) Where you are Heading.

Your chosen terminal is very crucial when analysing a situation. It determines which essential procedures you have to follow so as to reach where you want to go. If you want to build a home, you start by drawing a sketch, an actual drawing then draw a complete picture of how you want the home to be. We are not an option too. In life, we must have a blue print of what we want to attain.

(4)Recognize your privi-leges.

Every situation is always accompanied by priv-ileges only that many people fail to recognize their privileges. Look at Hanna in the bible. She was countered with a situation that involved two great afflictions Which were huge intimi-dations to her life. She had very restricted mastery over the first and none over the other. She was in a polygamous marriage with her core wife Peninnah who was a cutthroat. Over and above, Peninnah disliked her a big deal. Secondly, Hanna could not bear children due to her barrenness. As you know, this situation can be so bothering for any lady who wants to bear children to her husband. But to her dur-ing that time, it was a fountain of severe agony and blow. These two confrontations obsessed her day and night since Peninnah did everything within her capacity to haunt her. But Hanna never forgot her privileges. And this is what helped her to survive and cope with the situation, finally succeeding and overcoming the challenges. Hanna was humble regardless of the repulsive things Peninnah used to do to her. She was her husband's favourite, she had faith in God but most importantly she knew how to pray. When she went down on her knees and called upon God, He heard her prayer. And God not only gave her a child, but also children. After Hanna was blessed with children, The bible doesn't mention the name of Peninnah anymore.

It doesn't matter what kind of a challenge you are facing in your situation; you will always find a privilege within it. Don't sleep, wake up from your comfort zone. Open your ears. Open your eyes. Look around, listen to the waves, realize your privileges, utilize them and get moving.

Strategic fall to fly 3

1. **Dream**

2. **Persist**

3. **Analyze your situation**

Mentorship

To succeed in life, a mentor is essential regard-less of your profession, field, and what you want to achieve. This is someone trusted and experienced who advises and helps you to achieve your goals and vision.

> A Mentor is like a mother. When you
> are scared, she encourages you.
> When you fall down, she lifts you.
> When you go astray, she corrects you.
> When you are misled, she advices
> you. And yet when you succeed, she
> applauds you.

Most organizations, school, and universities, usually offer formal mentoring programs. At times you will find that in these structured arrangements, mentors and mentees are assessed so that mentees can be matched with the right mentors, where as other organizations prefer that mentors and mentee be different. Either way, it's advisable to find someone whom you are comfortable with as far as advise is concerned. Someone whom you admire and respect will be a perfect match for you if you are finding a mentor on your own.

Figure out exactly what you need from the mentor and what skills you would like to develop with his or her assistance. In choosing a mentor, remember that your goals and objectives are of significant importance.

Discovering a Mentor

A good mentor wishes to work with someone they respect and admire, also their passion of success. If the mentor wishes to model you in their own image, it could be fine as long as the mentor is not too enslaving about it and you are comfortable with that.

Remember, a mentor can as well be your role model. But these are two different things. A lot of folks confuse these two. A role model is someone whom you desire and admire their image, even though you may never get an opportunity to meet. They are not available for you. While a mentor is someone who is always available for you any time. Nevertheless, if you admire your mentor's image, you can let the mentor be your role model. You don't need to tell the mentor about this if you don't wish to. You can keep it to yourself.

It's important to have a series of meetings with the person you are considering for a mentor after which you will be able to tell him or her that you prefer to have them as your mentor.

Avoid a mentor who is too predominant, a know it all and reckoning. Look for an affirmative attitude, resilient and a person who will celebrate your success and be worried by your failure.

Make sure you build trust in your mentor by being open. Share your achievements and failures with him or her and in case of any misfire don't keep it to yourself. Let your mentor know the course and also be ready to accept any mistakes which may occur. A mentor should also be ready and willing to learn from you too.

What a Mentor can offer

If you have a mentor in the same organisation, the mentor can be so instrumental to you. He or she can help you sail through the office politics and gossips. Again, the mentor can introduce you to the senior management and maybe recommend you for a promotion.

The main work of a mentor is to assess your strengths and weaknesses and foster a sense of belonging so as to ignite the motion. A mentor can help you come up with a different way of dealing with challenges that's why it's advisable to find a mentor who is more of an instructor than an advisor, and indeed a mentor who inaugurates your decision-making channels by offering alternatives rather than apprising you what to carry out.

Advisory relationship

Agree with your mentor about mutual expectations and understanding for the relationship. The way it will work and what it will look like but most importantly how frequently you will meet or communicate. Again, this relationship needs absolute acmes of care so that it can bear fruits of the highest quality.

Just the same way you would cultivate your garden and take care of the crops so as to produce healthy and quality products, so is the advisory relationship. From the word go, both of you should come up with a way of terminating the relationship without any hard feelings at all.

Never overload your mentor by requiring a lot of time and assiduity or perhaps becoming wholly depended on him or her. Many times, the mentor may offer a lot more than you do to the relationship. Always appreciate by praising his or her benefaction to your growth. Also show that you value his or her counselling.

The awareness of being in demand and changing one's life will often be a rewarding upshot for the mentor, you can also surprise your mentor with a gift of appreciation. It could be a watch, a pen or even a note of praise to the mentor.

Strategic fall to fly 4

1. **Dream**
2. **Persist**
3. **Analyze your situation**
4. **Find a mentor**

Personal branding

This sets the difference between success and failure. It involves doing extraordinary things and earning the moral Authority of the public.

Remember it's not easy to be a personal brand If you don't know how to get along with people. You must have a clear way of approaching all types of people. Love is the key word. With love you can change a life, bring a smile and most likely achieve what you want. Love the young ones because they possess the Kingdom of Heaven. Love the needy because no one values them.

Love the wealthy for they are yet to learn more things and lastly, Love the aged for they possess the wisdom. Personal branding stands on these three cardinal pillars:

- **Attitude**

- **Discipline**

- **Stress**

```
 1                                              A
 2                                              B
 3                                              C
 4                                              D
 5     1 20 20  9 20  21  4  5                   E
 6   A T  T  I  T  U   D  E    100% SUCCESS OR FAILURE  F
 7                                              G
 8                                              H
 9     4  9 19  3  9  16 12  9 14 5              I
10   D I  S  C  I  P   L  I  N  E    100% SUCCESS  J
11                                              K
12                                              L
13                                              M
14                                              N
15    19 20 18  5 19  19                         O
16   S  T  R  E  S   S       100% GAIN TO SUCCEED  P
17                                              Q
18                                              R
19                                              S
20                                              T
21                                              U
22                                              V
23                                              W
```

Attitude

Your attitude determines 100% your success or failure. The way you view things is very important. If your attitude is positive towards everyone and everything, you are likely to get a positive response, a positive outcome, and even a positive end. Let anyone you meet detect your positive attitude.

Discipline

Just like necessity is the mother of invention, discipline is the mother of success. It's pretty hard to succeed without discipline. Discipline your thoughts, actions, behaviour, relationships, words, feelings, time health, and even power. Discipline determines 100% your success. Let anyone you meet recognise you out of your discipline.

Stress

You have heard people say a lot of times that without pain there is no gain. Again, being a public figure, you will face a lot of rejection and resistance from those who don't like you. Be prepared for this but most importantly remain firm and keep shaping your image.

"Sometimes it takes a painful experience to make us change our ways". **PROVERBS 20:30**

Many people do succeed when they are in the middle of Darkness. When things are very hard and pressure mounting from each corner. When nothing seems to lead to the other. This is when the fortuity appears.

> Darkness attracts light and light always follow darkness

Strategic fall to fly 5

1. **Dream**

2. **Persist**

3. **Analyze your situation**

4. **Find a mentor**

5. **Brand yourself**

Potential explosion

This is the ability to bring out a hidden or dormant trait out of an individual. Every man and woman have some potential to be admired. But most of them stay hidden and locked up in themselves. Not unless they are unleashed, they might stay and rot in there.

This calls for a wake-up note to any person who wishes to succeed. You need to realize and act on your hidden potential.

Page | 103

"Every individual has a place to fill in the world, and is important in some respect, whether he chooses to be or not"

-*NATHANIEL HANTHORN*

We are all great since we come from one great

father. God Almighty.

"The world and all that is in it belongs to the Lord."
PSALMS 24:1

The earth and all those who live in it are His.

We all belong to him and he loves us equally.

Think of a father who loves his children

equally. He always makes sure

that his children get equal portions of their in-

heritance. The difference comes out in the way

the children use their portions. Some multi-

plies the value of what they get and make dou-

ble or triple, others maintain what they receive

while others consume and finish the little, they

receive. And by the end of the day, you will

find that even though everyone got equal

portions, they all stand at different status of possession. Not because either of them was favoured but because of their behaviour.

Unleash your greatness

"Never before was there a being like you"

-DEL CARNAGE

Among the wonderful work that God did and again in the history of creation, man is the greatest of all. Created in the image and likeness of God, and given power over all the other creations Including the earth and soil which bears his name, to work on it and make it productive.

"Then God said. And now we will make human beings, they will be like us and resemble us. They will have power over the fish, the birds, and all the animals. Domestic and wild. Large and small" GENESIS 1:26

So, God created human beings making them look like him. He created them male and female Blessed them and spoke.

"Have many children so that your descendants will live all over the earth and bring it under their control. Am putting you in charge of the fish, the birds, and all the Wild animals" GENESIS 9:7

Man was therefore given power over everything which God placed on earth. The Bible says he was also blessed such that everything that he decided to do as long as it was in line with the moral values would be successful.

Again, since we possess God's image, we should also resemble him both in character and thoughts. God is creative and innovative. He created man first and later on, he made a woman out of the man. This was the greatest innovation ever which man has never and will never emerge to even though we have been given the capability. We should follow what our Great father did by being innovative too.

Let's look at it from this perspective. If a man can make clay that bears his name productive, what of other things which were put under his total absolute control.? Many people know that they are capable of doing great things but do nothing about it. They forget that God has already blessed everything that a man decides to do as long as it pleases God. While others fail to know where to begin and where to end. Here is the way to get moving:

(a). Love yourself

Mankind is the nature's greatest miracle with great characters and admirable appearances. It doesn't matter your position in society. And regardless of your status, education, and family background. You are important and God made you with a reason and for a purpose.

"I chose you before I gave you life, and before you were born, I selected you to be a prophet to the nations"
JEREMIAH 1:5

In whichever place you are, and whatever thing you do, just know that it's not by chance but you were selected a long time ago to carry out your task in fulfilling your purpose.

Be yourself at all times and do what you feel. Don't imitate simply because you want to look like someone else. Be a pioneer of your plans and styles even if they have existed before.

Again, don't just do a thing simply because you want to make others happy. Do it because you feel it contributes to your success and happiness.

"I don't know the key to success, but the key to failure is trying to impress everyone"
- Bill Cosby

Show gratitude to God by appreciating yourself the way you are and even making the best out of yourself.

(b). Hang on your dream.

For you to dream, you have to sleep. But re-member, you have to wake up out of your comfort zone and face the music as it is.

Set your own goals and own them. If you go out to the street and ask everyone about their dreams you will get some people who even have a million dreams. Simply because every-one wishes to grow better than they are today. But the difference comes in when you fail to own your dream. How deep have you dug in to it and how deep do you still have to dig so as to reach it.

(C). Think positively

You must talk and wish yourself good things. Most likely what you wish for yourself will come true. What you wish for yourself, is what your heart desires and that is what God will grant to you.

"Then you will call to me. You will come and pray to me and I will answer you" JEREMIAH 29:12

Don't tolerate force friends and company. They only ruin your morals and kill your dreams before setting themselves aside to watch your next move. If they oppose you, gain more power and move on with your plans' Carnage puts it clear that; *no one kicks a dead dog*: This means that if they fight you, whatever you are doing is very much alive and worthwhile. Don't give the devil a chance to win. Press until the going gets better.

"The power of an idea is measured by the degree of re-sistance it attracts"
      -David Yotto

If you start something and get no resistance, that means what you are doing is not alive at all. But if you get a million rebels, merry and keep the fire burning. Just keep in mind that soon or later, success will be yours.

(D). Love your work

Having passion in your work is a very essential step towards achieving your dream. It is not possible to fail in something you love with passion.

A farmer in Brazil was having a field that was surrounded by many other fields. His field was ever green and all the time his harvest was ample. In fact, his produce alone used to be more than all the other fields combined together.

Then one day there was an audit by the Agricultural Association. After going through his past records, the auditors were so amazed and congratulated him so much for the excellent production he has had.

He was angry and disappointed. "Why do you look sad.? It's a good compliment concerning your field's performance.?" One of the Auditors asked the farmer worriedly. "I love what I do," said the farmer. And continued. "Yes, there are many challenges that I encounter on a daily basis, but they never bother me at all. I know how to go about them. I have never failed in farming and I will never fail. That's my believe. Farming is my passion. You should have simply said; "you love your work," the farmer said smilingly.

"Do all your work in love"1 CORINTH 16:14.

(E). Expedite

Yes, it has never happened in your life. it only happens to others in your sight. But you will make it happen. It is your turn now. You have all it takes to make your dreams come true.

You may not possess great riches and wealth, but you are a great achiever, a great performer and most importantly a great successful person. Everyone in this world can make to be what they want in life. Reach their desired destination and be happy. The difference comes in the different categories of people.

All the people of the world lie in three main categories in terms of performance.

(A). Those who wait for things to happen. They like sitting down and watching others as they achieve their goals, but they refuse to get up and do something concerning their lives. They underrate themselves and limit themselves to such an extent that even the simplest thing is hard for them. This category of people never leave behind a legacy even though they possess the potential.

(B). There is also another category of people who usually don't know what is happening around them and what is going on with their lives. They are just there and they live life the way it is. They never do anything to change their lives either positively or even negatively. They never get hot or cold. To them everything is always right.

(c). The last category of people is known as the 'champions.' They are extraordinary people because they make what is impossible

possible. They achieve what they desire and they fulfil their purpose. They make things happen.

They have no comparison because the only thing which can be compared to them is their achievement. They never feel complacent and all the time they always have a goal to achieve. They refuse to remain in their comfort zone and choose to go through the rough road. Up the hills and down the valleys to get what they want. They take risk just like a normal exercise. For them darkness is nothing but light to their destination. As an individual, ask yourself; "which category do I belong.?"

Every morning the eagle wakes up and flies high in the sky. And from a very far away distance it sports several tiny animals and birds on the land. It identifies the most confused among them and sees potential food. It then prepares well and goes down for it. Otherwise, it will stay hungry the whole day. Over and above, the eagle does not limit itself to anything. even in its old age when many get tired, and Weary, the eagle flies very high in the deep skies and goes through the process of rejuvenation. This is a very painful process for the eagle. It involves scratching and rubbing it's body on hard and rough surfaces until the old body is gone and the eagle becomes new again.

Many people who fail in life, fear going through hardships, experiencing new challenges and facing the truth.

The only formula of success; Know your targets, your limits, where you fit and where you don't. But most importantly know if you are an eagle or something else which has got no description or even traits to be admired.

Strategic fall to fly 6

1. **Dream**
2. **Persist**
3. **Analyze your situation**
4. **Find a mentor**
5. **Brand yourself**
6. **Explore your potential**

HAVE A CLEAR VISION

All people have eyes, but not everyone have vision. While the dictionary offers several definitions of vision, I believe this is the ability to make great plans for the future. A picture in your imagination and most precisely to have a sight of your mind. You could be wise and clever, holding a big position in society and even achieve the acmes of academic ratings. But if you don't have a vision, you are as blind as a person who has never gone to school. It doesn't matter whether you are poor or rich, down or up, it doesn't matter whether you are young or old. A vision is necessary for any person who wants to succeed and raise their bar.

Draft your vision

You might have a tremendous plan but if you don't write it down on paper, it means nothing. You must write down your vision. This is the outset of owning the vision. It doesn't matter how huge and expensive your vision is, just write it down.

Many people do lose hope when they realize that their vision is a big-ticket. Giving up should not be the option at all if you are look-ing forward for success. Others give up when they realize that their vision is too big and might take a long time. Again, giving up is not the option. Or just having the vision on your mind is not enough.

There is more than that in a black and white statement.

"Put it in writing, because it is not yet time for it to come true. But the time is coming quickly, and what I show you will come true. It may seem slow in coming, but wait for it; it will certainly take place, and it will not be delayed." HABAKKUK2:3

How to write your vision

To write down your vision excellently, you must come up with a good plan. The underlying procedure will help you come up with a good plan:

(1). Believe in God

Trust in God and ask him to guide your vision. Pray to God for guidance and He will lead you. Commit every plan to him and you will be successful.

"Ask the Lord to bless your plans and you will be successful in carrying them out" PROVERBS 16:3

(2). Explore yourself by defining:

The real you

You are a unique creature with unique features and characters. You are all you need to be what you want to be. No one knows you better than yourself.

Define whom you think you are and write it down.

Your Origin

Here you define your past encounters highlighting your failures and achievements. And also, your current status. By so doing, you get to know where to start and where to end. It also helps you to know where to change and what to stop.

The direction you are heading

You can't just leave your house without knowing where you are heading to or where you
want to go. Life is a journey and you must plan
and arrange the itinerary for your desired destination. If you don't do so you will hover at
the brinks of wishing all of your life. You must
know what you want to achieve and have a
blueprint of your future. Define your destination.

Reason for your existence

No one exists by chance or by opportunity. We
were all created by God for a purpose and with
a reason. And so never should you think you
are worthless or less important. David was the
youngest amongst his brothers. And so, no one
recognized and thought of him being the King

of Israel. But God chose him and made him powerful.

The same thing applies to us. At times you can be neglected and isolated because of your status in society. But this should not burr you from getting to where you want to go. Jacob knew Joseph as a good son. The brothers knew him as a useless dreamer. The travellers looked at Joseph and saw in him a slave. Potiphar knew Joseph as a good servant. Potiphar's wife identified Joseph as a potential lover. The prison officers knew him as a prisoner. All these people were very wrong. From the word go, God had chosen him as a prime minister of Egypt.

Don't be discouraged by what people see in you. Remember David got the anointing of becoming a King of Israel while he was a simple child herding sheep and goat. Esther was a simple orphaned girl yet she was a Queen in waiting. So, it doesn't matter how people see you, but it matters a lot how God sees you.

How close you are to God

When we mention the name of God some people think it's a name just like any other name. But God is great than you can ever imagine.

"Heaven is my throne and the earth is my footstool. What kind of a house then can you build for me? What kind of a place for I to live in.? I created the whole universe! Am pleased with those who are humble. And repentant., who fear me and obey me"
ISAIA 66:1

There is no one, there is nothing ever that is greater than God.

"All the gold and Silver of the world is mine."

HAGGAI 2:8

If your relationship with God is good, he will grant you what you wish to have. Decide to be close to God and declare to obey his commandments, and you will be shocked by what he will do to your life.

"If you obey the Lord your God, and faithfully keep all his commandments, that I am giving you today, he will make you greater than any other nation on earth."

DEUTERONOMY 28:1

YOUR VISION.

To come up with your clear vision, there are several things you have to Consider. This will depend on how you feel towards a particular thing. In other words, the bigger picture of your life.

Identify your Passion

What is that one thing that you never get bored or tried to do. What is that one thing that defines your favourite space. That one thing that drives you crazy even when every other thing sounds like ugly noise to you. What do you love doing over and over again.

Define your Legacy

Every great man and woman leaves behind a heritage in terms of performance, Development, and achievement. What would you like to be remembered for? What would you like your wife and kids to say about you? What about your society and the world at large.

Define your mission statement

Come up with a compendium of everything that you want to do. Arrange them in order of priority but most importantly put them in black and white.

Define your vision statement

A lot of folks. Almost everyone confuse between a mission and a vision. While a mission is a summary of everything that you intend to do in the future, a vision remains as a total blue print of what you want to achieve. Summarise what you exactly want to do in just a few words. One or two sentences.

Remain principled.

Having a vision is being responsible and to be responsible, you must have very clear principles to guide you at all time. Adhere to your principles.

your goals and objectives

These are detailed steps necessary to fulfilling your vision. A goal is a dream with a deadline. To be successful in life, you must dream and make your dream a real one, set time frames. Break the goal into smaller parts and describe how to get to the goal. Highlight means and ways of achieving your goal. These are the objectives.

There are several goals depending on one's priority. Don't set goals higher than your grasp. You know yourself well. You know where you come from and where you want to go. You know what you are capable of and what you are not capable of. So, sit down and be in your fresh state of mind as you come up with your real goals and preview them daily, weekly, monthly, and annually.

Once you achieve a certain goal, set other higher goals. You could set a variety of goals ranging from spiritual goals to financial goals among others:

- **Spiritual goals**
- **Family goals**
- **Health goals**
- **Financial Goals**
- **Investment goals**

Among other types of goals which you can set as you achieve the first ones.

Strategic fall to fly 7

1. **Dream**
2. **Persist**
3. **Analyze your situation**
4. **Find a mentor**
5. **Brand yourself**
6. **Explore your potential**
7. **Have a vision-write down your vision**

The bitter truth in action

Every truth has bitterness in it. A lot of people never like to hear the truth even from the right source. But this is the only thing that can set you free and even pave a way for your success.

Below are some bitter truths which when put into action will help you in achieving your goal:

Remain to be yourself.

 Many people pretend to be different from what they are. This is what brings about the confusion. It makes you lose your stand and wander here and there aimlessly. Simply be a product of your design.

Keep Learning.

The five years that King Nebuchadnezzar stayed in the forest eating grass like an animal was the most daring experience he ever had in his entire life. But at the end of it all, he learned to respect God. Again, Jonah had to stay in the womb of a fish for three days. That was too a daring experience. But he also learned to obey God's voice. Life never stops teaching us. So, learn from every single move you make. Learn from any single person you meet. Learn from any single site you visit but

most importantly learn from mistakes and experiences.

Be of value to the people around you

Be someone whom people can rely on, believe
in, trust, and also respect. But most importantly help people grow together with You.
Don't be mean to others. Be kind and life will
be kind to you too.

Don't brag with money.

Remember being wealthy is not having a lot of
money or even being educated. It's simply giving out what you have in the only way you
deem suitable. A good example of this is the
story of two sons who went to their father
with conflict of a donkey.

Their donkeys resembled each other but the eldest son had his donkey marked for identification. The young son had lost his donkey and claimed that his brother had taken his. But when they went to the father, He threatened to slaughter the donkey in question.

The son who had lost his donkey accepted without any hard feeling but the real owner of the donkey requested the father to give it to his brother instead. Then the father realized that the donkey belonged to his elder son.

The elder son gave out what he had and by so doing, he got total absolute justice in return. At times we will be forced to offer what we have so that we can do away with extreme challenges in life.

Many people don't like giving out hence losing out valuable and important things and opportunities in life. One day when Jesus was preaching in the streets, a young man ran to him and called, "teacher, what can I do in order to possess the kingdom of heaven.?" Jesus told him, "Obey Gods commandments. Do not lie, do not steal, do not kill among others". He said to Jesus. "I have always done that my Lord." Then Jesus looked at him and loved him. "Go and sell all your belongings and give all the money to the poor then come and follow me. if you do that you will of no doubt, possess the kingdom of God" The young man turned worriedly and never followed Jesus again hence losing the valuable kingdom of heaven.

How many times have we lost valuable opportunities and other things simply because we are mean? Give and you will also receive.

Be responsible for your life.

Take control of everything in your life including your moves, your success or failure, your relationships, your finances, your goals and achievements. Your feelings and any other thing related to you as a person.

Live life to your standard.

Always measure the depth of the waters before you can dive.

Don't live life which is above your standard. This will only lead to your struggles and perhaps downfall. Wear what fits you at a specific time.

Be flexible.

Life is a cycle of events. You don't know which event will befall you tomorrow and so you should always be prepared for whatever eventuality which might take place.

"Knowing is not enough; we must apply. Willing is not enough; we must do."
                    -JOHANN WOLFGANG VON GOETH

Strategic fall to fly 8

1. **Dream**

2. **Persist**

3. **Analyze your situation**

4. **Find a mentor**

5. **Brand yourself**

6. **Explore your potential**

7. **Have a vision-write down your vision**

8. **The bitter truth in action**

Plan to succeed

In our lives, there are moments of choice when we are surrounded on all sides by challenges, negative thoughts and possibilities. Our paths seem to be darkened and doomed. This is the time when many people lose focus and start worrying about other unnecessary things.

I will give example of an antelope that was expectant: In the heart of a dense forest, there lived a pregnant antelope eagerly awaiting the arrival of her little one. As the labor pains began, she realized she had not yet found a suitable place to give birth. Determined and with a sense of urgency, she ventured through the foliage, desperately seeking a safe haven.

After a while, the weary antelope stumbled upon a secluded grassy enclosure nestled within the bush. The contractions intensified, and she knew time was of the essence. However, her surroundings posed a myriad of threats. In one corner, a falconer stood with his arrow drawn, ready to strike. On another side, a hungry leopard lurked, mouth agape, hungry for its next meal. And to further complicate matters, a slithering python stealthily approached from a different direction. The situation seemed dire, and the antelope felt overwhelmed.

Yet, in the face of imminent danger, the pregnant antelope did something remarkable. She steadfastly ignored the perils that encircled her, choosing instead to focus solely on the paramount task at hand—bringing a new life into the world. Placing her unwavering trust in a higher power, she summoned all her strength and focused on the miracle unfolding within her.

Suddenly, as if summoned by her unwavering determination, a thunderstorm erupted out of nowhere. The fierce winds and torrential rain bewildered the falconer, causing his arrow to miss its mark and strike down the leopard. In the same instant, a blinding bolt of lightning flashed before the falconer's eyes, rendering him momentarily blinded and disoriented. And as if responding to the antelope's unwavering faith, the python silently slipped away into the depths of the forest.

With the dangers vanquished, the antelope peacefully brought forth her precious offspring into the world. A healthy, vibrant new life emerged, thanks to the mother's unwavering focus and belief in a higher power. Had she allowed fear and confusion to cloud her judgment, she might have sprinted aimlessly, putting herself and her unborn child at risk. But she remained resolute, focusing on her priority with unwavering determination.

This tale reminds us of the incredible power that lies within us when we steadfastly pursue our goals, undeterred by the challenges and distractions that surround us. It teaches us the importance of staying focused on what truly matters, even when faced with overwhelming obstacles. And above all, it illustrates the transformative force of unwavering faith, guiding us through the darkest of times and leading us to extraordinary outcomes.

Sometimes when challenges come our way, we lose focus hence losing our destiny.

Planning to succeed is simply focusing on your purpose, ignoring all the other things, especially challenges dealing with them easily, directing your faith to God and trusting in His mighty powers. Below are a few steps essential to planning successfully.

(a). Appreciate your creator.

Always thank God for everything. Just everything. Worship him and keep aside his tithe and 10% of every earning.

"Bring all the full amount of tithe to my storehouse and taste me says the Lord"
MALACHI 3:10

 If you give to the Lord, he will never let you lack. Also, practice the art of giving even to others so that you may also receive.

(b) Appreciate yourself.

Treat yourself once in a while. Enjoy with the people you prioritize especially your family. But remember every % you spent, save the same percentage. Do not let the saved per-centage be stagnant. Instead let it multiply its value. Venture in to other sources of income and make sure that your priority is achieved. It's safe and adds value to your life.

A certain man from Europe embarked on a memorable African adventure with his beloved wife and two children. They opted to stay at a remarkable hotel called G-Durex Hotel, im-mersing themselves in the rich beauty of the continent for an extended period of over three months. During their stay, the man found himself engaged in a conversation with the assertive and curious hotel general manager, who sought to uncover the secret behind the family's apparent financial ease and tranquility.

With a calm smile, the man met the manager's gaze and proceeded to share his perspective. "Mr. Flower," he began, "I may not be exceptionally wealthy, but I have indeed planned for success." He proceeded to explain his approach, shedding light on the steps he had taken to ensure financial stability and peace of mind. His words conveyed a simple yet powerful strategy that guided his financial decisions.

The man revealed that he had diligently saved for this holiday over an extended period of time. Every time he received 20 pennies, he set aside 3 for his holiday fund and another 3 for his personal savings account. However, he didn't stop there. Prior to embarking on the journey, he astutely transformed his savings into strategic investments. By doing so, he ensured that even while on holiday, his financial endeavors continued to thrive, thereby enhancing the quality of his life.

It was this meticulous planning and foresight that allowed him to enjoy his time at the Durex Hotel without succumbing to financial worry or panic. His investments were actively generating income, bolstering his confidence in the stability of his business. This mindset provided him with a sense of security and tranquility, allowing him to fully immerse himself in the joys of the African experience.

This tale reminds us of the power of prudent financial planning and the value of investing in our future. The man's approach exemplified the importance of setting aside resources for both present enjoyment and long-term growth. Through his thoughtful actions, he demonstrated how strategic decisions can create a ripple effect, enriching our lives even during times of relaxation and exploration.

(C) Cut down your cost.

"a budget tells us what we can afford but doesn't keep us from buying it"

   -WILLIAM FEATHER.

Cut down the cost of your living. If you are eager to achieve your dream. As you budget your income, remember that there is no big or small money. If you cannot manage the little you have, then you will not be able to manage more than you expect.

(D) Don't let go of your opportunity.

Any opportunity you come across is not worthy losing. Hold on to it. utilize it and make it your bridge to your success. Do not let any opportunity slip away from your hand.

In the chronicles of ancient times, a tale unfolded about a man named Jacob who found himself embroiled in a profound disagreement with his brother Esau. The intensity of their conflict led Jacob to make a difficult decision: he chose to flee, seeking solace and a fresh start along the path before him.

As he embarked on his journey, the universe had a remarkable encounter in store for him. Jacob crossed paths with a mysterious figure, and a battle ensued between them, lasting through the night. The strength and resilience of the man Jacob faced revealed that he was no ordinary being; he was none other than an angel—a celestial messenger of God.

As dawn approached, Jacob's realization dawned upon him. He discerned the divine nature of the being before him. In that moment, resolute and determined, Jacob reached out and firmly grasped the angel, determined not to release him without receiving a blessing. With unwavering faith and conviction, he boldly declared his intent to the celestial visitor.

Moved by Jacob's steadfast faith and unyielding determination, the angel acquiesced. He bestowed upon Jacob a profound blessing, accompanied by a transformative act: he changed Jacob's name to Israel. This divine renaming symbolized a profound shift in Jacob's destiny. From that point forward, he would be known as Israel—the father of a great nation.

Jacob's descendants would go on to form the twelve tribes of Israel, establishing a legacy that would shape the course of history. It was through Jacob's unwavering resolve, his refusal to let go of the angelic messenger until he received the blessing, that his path took a remarkable turn. By embracing the challenge and holding on to the divine presence before him, Jacob secured the blessings that would shape his destiny and that of his descendants for generations to come.

This timeless tale serves as a testament to the power of faith, resilience, and unwavering determination. Jacob's unwavering grip symbolizes his unyielding commitment to seeking blessings and embracing the divine intervention in his life. It encourages us to hold steadfast in the face of challenges and to persistently pursue our dreams and aspirations. Just as Jacob's encounter altered the course of his existence, so too can our unwavering faith and determination shape our own destinies, leading us to incredible blessings and fulfilling journeys.

Sometimes we come across many opportunities in life and we let them vanish either knowingly or unknowingly. Some of these opportunities come in form of formidable challenges just the same way the angel was tough to Jacob. And not unless we realize, it becomes very hard for us to accept or appreciate the opportunity. It could be that new job you have landed and your boss is on your neck. It could be that business you have just ventured and instead of getting profit you are recording a loss. This is a challenge to loosen your laces but instead, tighten them. Be ready to grab the opportunity. Yes, you could be shaken much and scared a lot but make sure you excel with the acmes of prosperity.

"Many of life's failures are people who did not realize how close they were to success when they gave up."

-THOMAS EDISON

Keep pressing and don't close your eyes even for a single minute. Even at the darkest hour, success might pass you and it may not come back again. Put some pressure on each and every corner so that you have an idea of suc-cess. Be out of your comfort zone knowing that success is a procedure and a process of sheer pressure and discomfort.

A story is given about a falconer who ventured into the depths of a lush forest, his heart set on a successful hunt. To his delight, fortune smiled upon him, and he managed to capture a graceful dove in his hands. The dove, sensing its fate drawing near, implored the falconer for mercy, offering him a promise of wisdom and

profound truths that could shape his life forever.

Initially skeptical, the falconer dismissed the
dove's entreaties, convinced that its words
were nothing more than a futile attempt to
avoid its inevitable destiny. However, the dove
persisted, assuring the falconer that its insights
held immense value and could greatly benefit
him.

Intrigued, the falconer relented, curious to
hear the four revelations the dove claimed to
possess. With a glimmer of hope in its eyes,
the dove began to share its wisdom. The first
lesson it imparted was a reminder to cherish
and retain the knowledge and experiences one
encounters throughout life. It urged the

falconer never to be forgetful but to hold onto the wisdom gained from what had been heard and witnessed.

The second truth revealed by the dove emphasized the importance of safeguarding the blessings and opportunities already in one's possession. It urged the falconer to hold tightly onto these precious gifts, recognizing their inherent value and potential for personal growth and fulfillment.

The third insight conveyed by the dove served as a gentle reminder not to yearn for what is absent. It cautioned against longing and despairing over what one lacks, instead encouraging contentment and appreciation for the blessings already present in one's life.

The falconer eagerly awaited the revelation of the fourth and final truth that promised to be life-changing. However, the dove set forth a condition—the falconer must release it before it could disclose this transformative insight. Filled with trepidation, the falconer acqui-esced, setting the dove free to perch upon a nearby tree.

As the dove settled in its newfound freedom, it posed a question to the falconer, inquiring about the first and second lessons it had shared. The falconer recollected the wisdom imparted—never to forget and to hold onto what is already in one's hands.

Yet, with a heavy heart, the falconer realized that he had forgotten the very teachings the dove had instilled while it was cradled in his hands. Overwhelmed with regret, he wept, succumbing to his forgetfulness and relinquishing the precious dove—a vessel containing a piece of pure gold.

The dove's final lesson resonated deeply. It highlighted the falconer's failure to heed the earlier teachings, demonstrating the folly of crying over what one has lost when it was in their power to retain it. The falconer realized the profound truth that had been offered to him, and with a sense of enlightenment, he vowed to apply these lessons to his life moving forward.

This timeless tale reminds us of the significance of cherishing what we possess, cultivating gratitude for the blessings already bestowed upon us, and being mindful of the wisdom we encounter. It underscores the importance of being attentive and present in our lives, ensuring that we do not allow precious opportunities to slip away due to forgetfulness or discontentment. Ultimately, the tale serves as a poignant reminder to treasure the invaluable insights that can shape our existence and empower us to lead lives of purpose and fulfillment.

(E) Take risk

"what kind of man would live where there is no danger? I don't believe in taking foolish chances. But nothing can be accomplished by not taking a chance at all." Charles Lindbergh.

In the early days of aviation, Amelia Earhart, with her indomitable spirit and passion for flying, she captivated the world and etched her name into the annals of history. Amelia, or "Melia" as her friends affectionately called her, had a dream that seemed audacious and daring for a time when women were expected to stay at home and tend to domestic duties.

Amelia Earhart attended college at Columbia University in New York City, where she studied pre-med. However, her interest in aviation led her to change her focus and pursue a career in flying. To finance her flying lessons, Amelia worked various jobs, including as a photographer, a truck driver, and a stenographer.

She also joined the American Red Cross during World War I, where she worked as a nurse's aide and later as a volunteer in a military hospital. These experiences exposed her to aircraft and sparked her fascination with flying.

She grew up in Atchison, Kansas, and from a young age, she was enthralled by the sight of airplanes soaring through the sky. She was determined to become a pilot and face the open skies with courage and grace. Despite the societal constraints placed upon women, Amelia persevered and embarked on a journey that would change her life and inspire generations to come.

In 1920, Amelia took her first flying lesson and immediately fell in love with the sensation of being airborne. She worked odd jobs to save money for her flying lessons, eagerly absorbing every aspect of aviation theory and practice. Amelia's dedication paid off, and in 1923, she became only the sixteenth woman in the world to earn a pilot's license.

With her newfound qualification, Amelia didn't rest on her laurels. She had a hunger for adventure that could not be satiated easily. In 1928, she received a phone call that would forever shape her destiny. It was an offer to become the first woman to fly across the Atlantic

Ocean. Melia jumped at the opportunity, part-
nering with pilot Wilmer "Bill" Stultz and copi-
lot Louis E. "Slim" Gordon.

On June 17, 1928, Amelia Earhart embarked on
the journey of a lifetime. The tiny red and gold
airplane, named the "Friendship," soared into
the sky, carrying her dreams and aspirations
along with it. Battling storms, turbulence, and
exhaustion, Amelia and her crew pressed on.
Twenty hours and forty minutes later, the
"Friendship" touched down in Burry Port,
Wales, making Amelia Earhart the first woman
to fly across the Atlantic.

Her achievement was celebrated worldwide,
and Amelia's courageous spirit only grew
stronger. She aimed higher, setting her sights
on becoming the first woman to fly solo across
the Atlantic Ocean. On May 20, 1932, Amelia

took off from Harbour Grace, Newfoundland, in her Lockheed Vega 5B aircraft named "The Friendship." With relentless determination, she flew through treacherous weather and navigational challenges, battling fatigue and doubt.

After an arduous flight lasting nearly 15 hours, Amelia Earhart triumphantly landed in Derry, Northern Ireland. Her feat shattered records, and she proved that women could conquer the skies just as bravely as men. Amelia became an international icon, inspiring countless women to pursue their dreams fearlessly.

Amelia's unparalleled passion for flying didn't stop there. She set her sights on circumnavigating the globe, a journey that would test her skills, endurance, and unwavering spirit. On

June 1, 1937, she embarked on her fateful final flight, departing from Miami, Florida, with her navigator, Fred Noonan, by her side.

As they made their way across the vast Pacific Ocean, a series of unforeseen challenges plagued their mission. Tragically, on July 2, 1937, Amelia Earhart's plane disappeared near Howland Island, an uninhabited coral island in the central Pacific Ocean. Despite extensive search efforts, no trace of Amelia, Fred, or their aircraft was ever found.

The loss of Amelia Earhart was a profound blow to the aviation community and the world at large. However, her legacy endures.

Strategic fall to fly 9

1. **Dream**

2. **Persist**

3. **Analyze your situation**

4. **Find a mentor**

5. **Brand yourself**

6. **Explore your potential**

7. **Have a vision-write down your vision**

8. **The bitter truth in action**

9. **Plan to succeed**

Choose Wisely

The choice is a point in time when one is involved in decision-making. This can as well include determining the credits of several options and choosing one or more of them. One can choose between thought up options (in the event ...) and authentic options followed by the kindred action. For instance, a tourist may choose an itinerary for an excursion hinged on the first choice of arriving at a given terminal as soon as possible. Either way whichever choice you make in life not only does it matter a lot but it also maps your destiny.

"Attitude is a choice. Happiness is a choice. Giving is a choice. Respect is a choice. Whatever choice you make, makes you Choose wisely"

-ROY. T. BONNET

There is a short story on how choice makes you whom you are hence determining your destiny. It's about a King who lived long time ago. He was rich. Many knew him for his impeccable administration and for ruling the hearts of his lessons. People would go to him with all sorts of issue with high hopes and he would make sure that he solved their problems. Time passed, and the King become old and brittle. He began to worry about who would take over from him. And so, the question of who would be the scion to his cathedra started to dominate his mind. Luckily, the King had three sons who were loyal, obedient, and respectful to him and the Kingdom at large. He knew one of the three would take over from him, but he didn't know who exactly among the three of his sons had the real calibre fit to be a King. So, he decided to infuse a plan. He called the sons and accorded them $ 1000 each. Gave them a spell of five years to use these $ 1000. Then he said to them. Whoever brings a Diamond sheep for me shall be my successor. The three sons set out with their $1000. The eldest went to the town and rented a Durex room. Then he hired some men and women for him and send them to all corners of the land with the order to find a diamond sheep. After a few weeks, these men returned with nothing. In all of this process, his $1000 was finished. He lost the battle for the cathedra on the spot. The second son went to the town and started a shylock business. He earned a lot of profit from the shylock business and with the Money he had accumulated over the spell of five years, he gave the local metal smith to make a diamond sheep for him.

The youngest son had the greatest brains of all the sons. With the $1000, he build a small residential house for himself and started living in a swarm of poor and needy people. He invested his money in a business and got a lot of profit from it and thereby employed most of the citizens who worked under him. He not only employed the people, but he also build schools and hospitals out of the profit he made from his business. On seeing the impact, he had brought to their lives, the people started to treat him with loyalty and prominence. Appeased with his assignment, he went back to his father and told him that he had found the Diamond sheep he had requested them to find. He took his father around showing him the projects he had initiated and accomplished out of the$ 1000 he had given him. His father saw how the people treated his son with loyalty and prominence also the way they adored him, and he was very happy with what he saw in his son.

The five years came to an end and it was time for the three sons to stand before their father and present their diamond sheep. The firstborn had absolutely nothing to present or even tell his father because he had finished all his $ 1000 and he had not done anything tangible. The father was totally saddened with him. The second son stood in Infront of his father very confident and asked his men to bring along his diamond sheep. And sure, it was a statue of pure diamond which he had ordered from the local metalsmith. His father told him that was something but that wasn't the sheep he was expecting from him. When the turn came for the lastborn, he stood in Infront of his father, "Your Highness, please accept this sheep made of cotton. I ask you in all abasement not to underate the distinctive appeal of this sheep. I have framed it with my own hands. The hard work, travail, under the hot sun, to grow this cotton and the diligence put by the patriotic citizens of this great land is nothing less than diamond. When you send me to find a diamond sheep, a theorization appeared in my mind that the hearts of humans are more important and equal to the price of diamond". He said as he asked his men to bring and present a loyalty dress to his father.

"I managed to set up a cotton plantation and a processing factory which accommodates all of these patriotic citizens of our land as you can see." These words from the youngest of the king's sons sounded like candied song in the King's ears. Brought tears to the king's eyes as he felt and related himself to all the feelings of a common man vital for a king. Well merited, the cathedra was given to the young son for his aptitude and merits. His two brothers became his attendants.

"We all got both light and dark inside us. What matters is the part we choose to act on. that's who we are."

– GROWLING

This boy inspires many. Being the youngest in the family, he chose a path of his desire and the desire of his people. And a passion of his heart. He chose to work for the betterment of his society. And that's what he was sailing in waiting among other many things. There is a number of these which we must always be keen to make the appropriate choices in life:

Your words

The tongue is very powerful in many ways. Remember what you speak, how you put it, and who you speak it to matters a lot. The word of mouth is more powerful than you think. It can build or damage. It can raise or pull down. It can bring success or failure. Choose your words wisely.

"If your foot slips, you may recover your balance, but if your tongue slips, you may not recall your words" - MARTIN VANBEE.

Your thinking.

All that lingers in your mind, is a complete picture of who you are. You have a negative thought; your life becomes miserable. So, make sure that you always think and wish yourself well at all times because this is what makes you.

> *"As a man thinketh in his heart so he is"*
>   **PROVERBS 23:7**

Thinking well, straight, and positively is a very essential ingredient in the recipe for success.

"Raise against every negative thought that raises against you."
  -MATSHONA DHLIWAYO

Your character.

Character is what defines behaviour. If your character is pleasing, your behaviour is of course outstanding. Behaviour is all about vices and virtues. If you want to succeed in life, you must choose virtues over vices.

"Refuse the evil and choose to do well." ISAIAH 7:15

Your Time.

whom you spent time with, where you spent your time, and what you spent your time doing would result in your being productive or un-productive. Spent your time wisely and always make sure you spent time with people who add value to your life.

"Many people take no care of their money till they come nearly to the end of it. And others do just the same with their time.

-GOETH.

Remember that your success or failure lies in what you do with your time. Time is a para-mount ingredient in the recipe of success. Make good use of time and its fruits will not disappoint.

Your concurrence.

What you accept in life is a key thing you should choose wisely.

Don't ever accept everything that comes along. Measure what is before you before accepting. In other words, have a standard. If you feel you should say no, say it. Saying yes or no can easily change your destiny.

"Do not attempt to do a thing unless you are sure of yourself, but do not relinquish it simply because someone else is not sure of yourself."
        -STEWART WHITE

Your Friends.

friends play a very big role in one's Life and can either lift you or fail you. As they say, show me your friends and I tell you who you are. A person's status can be determined by the average of his friends. You must choose your friends wisely.

"God gives our relatives; thank Him we can choose our friends"   -ETHEL MUMFORD.

Research shows that social connections have a significant impact on our mental and physical health. Strong social support networks have been linked to lower rates of depression, anxiety, and other mental health issues. Additionally, people with strong social connections tend to have better physical health outcomes, such as lower rates of chronic illnesses and a longer life span.

Friendship and relationships are fundamental aspects of human life. They provide us with emotional support, companionship, and a sense of belonging. These connections play a vital role in our mental and physical health, and they can greatly impact our overall well-being.

Friendship remains to be one of the greatest investments in the world, but some friends are not worth having. They will drag you down day by day and you will never reach your destiny. Below is a list of the friends you should avoid with all your efforts and being because they are the kind of friends to drag you down every single day. They are the kinds of friends to land you in situations of regret and despair. Avoid them at all cost and this will save you from a lot of unnecessary situations.

The Goofy friends

These kinds of friends never take anything you plan with them seriously. To them nothing matters a lot. You are always a second option to them and they don't value you at all. Delete such kind of friends in your life.

The Fablers

These friends are pathological liars, and they never let you to know more about their life-style. Where they live or even work for that matter. You can never have a going concern together because they are never straight for-ward. Avoid them with all your being.

The Bloodsuckers

These friends are like parasites. They are like shadow because they only appear when the sun shines. When you have nothing to offer, they have no business to do with you. But they always rush to you when things go wrong on them. They never call to ask how you are faring on with life, but they call to report their issues to you. Avoid them and draw a line too.

Green-eyed Friends

When you move from grass to Grace, these friends are bitterly affected. They always look forward for your downfall. Nothing makes them happy than to see you perish.

The Betrayers

Even a python snake is not as dangerous as these friends. They merry with you on the table, but they bite you at night when you are asleep.

The Dark horses

These friends never get the concept of friendship because they are always competing with you. They see you with a Toyota today, tomorrow they buy a Subaru. You take your spouse on a holiday today tomorrow they want to do the same. They are always in a competition match with you.

Pong Friends

You go out with these friends and be ready to lose even important deals because they always start unnecessary drama. Throwing bottles, shouting and clapping hands. They disturb other customers with unnecessary noises and actions which can be so embarrassing to you as their friend.

Distraught Friends

These kinds of friends are always ready to throw a punch or two. They are very Violent and they don't care about Your health, safety, life and wellbeing. They can land you in to a very big problem due to their violent nature. Can you imagine being injured, arrested or even losing your life just because of a violent friend

Strategic fall to fly 10

1. Dream

2. Persist

3. Analyze your situation

4. Find a mentor

5. Brand yourself

6. Explore your potential

7. Have a vision-write down your vision

8. The bitter truth in action

9. Plan to succeed

10. Choose wisely

Manage your

Stress

Stress is the greatest killer disease. It curbs you from developing, chasing your goals and even succeeding.

If you are stressed either by your job or by something more personal, the first step to feeling better is to identify the course. Bellamy Flower who was a renowned professor and an occupational health expert in one of the world's great universities, said that in life everything can be fixed as long it's a real situation. Only imaginary situations are hard to deal with. Building ardent strength, being in a position to control the situation around you, having an excellent social connection and

affirming a definite angle in life are the open-
ers to good stress management.

I would therefore tell you about an OHS coach
who was teaching about stress management
principles to an auditorium full of professionals
who had come to further their knowledge on
Management and control systems. When she
raised up a jar of water, No one had the idea of
what she was going to do or say. Everyone
thought that she would advise them to take
enough water when faced with stress. On the
contrary, while smiling, the coach asked the
professionals. "What could be the weight of
this jar.?" The professionals gave out answers
ranging from different measurements. But she
replied, "From where I stand, the weight of
this jar is pointless. What matters is the time I
will hold it. In one hours, time, my hand will

definitely ache due to its weight and in a days' time, my arm will likely crick up and feel completely insensitive and paralysed pressuring me to drop the jar to the floor. Whichever the way, the weight of the jar remains constant, but the more time I hold it, the more burdensome it becomes." As the professionals in the auditorium shook their heads in agreement, she went on, "your anguish and stress are just like this jar. If they remain in your mind for a short spell, they will have no effect. If you extend the duration a bit longer, you will definitely ache. If you extent the duration for a whole day, you will completely be tired unless you drag them down."

Don't let today's stress cross over to tomorrow. Focus ahead and don't let any worry to curb your move towards your destiny. Having stress is not an issue, the issue is managing the stress. Below are some few additional things which you can do to maintain or manage your stress:

- *Always take time for yourself. Love your-self.*
- *Beware of your own Stress. Identify the course.*
- *Concentrate on controlling your own situation but not everybody's. This will stress you more and more.*
- *Daily exercise will burn off your stress chemicals. Put in consideration.*
- *Eat a lot of fruits and vegetables and drink a lot of water.*
- *Forgive others and take away the sorrow.*
- *Have fun. Don't limit yourself to fun because of stress.*

- *Identify stress. By so doing you will know how to deal with it.*
- *Keep a positive attitude. This will rouse your passion to move on.*
- *Manage your money well. Don't use it in unnecessary ways.*
- *Outdoor activities. Don't lock yourself in the house.*
- *Pray. This will allow you to have a divine connection with God.*
- *Quite smoking. This is one way of heading to the grave.*
- *Relationships nature and enjoy them. Don't ignore them.*
- *Sleep well. Buy yourself a comfortable mattress.*
- *Treat yourself once in a week.*
- *Try to understand things from the other person's point of view.*

- *Verify information from the source before exploding.*
- *Make regular retreat to your favourite space.*
- *Yearn for simplicity.*
- *Zest for life. Each day is a gift from God. Smile and be thankful that you are part and parcel of the bigger picture.*

Strategic fall to fly 11

1. **Dream**

2. **Persist**

3. **Analyze your situation**

4. **Find a mentor**

5. **Brand yourself**

6. **Explore your potential**

7. **Have a vision-write down your vision**

8. **The bitter truth in action**

9. **Plan to succeed**

10. **Choose wisely**

11. **Manage your stress**

Change your perspec-
tive

The way you see things. The way you think of things. The way you understand things and yet the way you take things is a very clear path to your destiny. If you think of things as worse, they will become so. If you want to move from grass to class, you must change the way you see things. I want to refer specifically to adversity. Because many people see adversity as the end game. Once tribulations come their way; they lose sight on the importance of life, and curse the day they were born. Some even commit suicide and others commit dangerous crimes which can land them in to bigger problems and even deny themselves chances of proving to the world that they are capable.

"Adversity is the first path to truth"

- LORD BYRON.

Failure is not the alternative to success, but it is for sure the path to success. Bill Gates is one of the world's richest people but he didn't earn his fortune in a straight line to success. To get into the entrepreneurial line, Bill Gates came up with Traf-o-Data, a company which he aimed at processing and analysing data from traffic tapes. Together with Paul Allen, his business partner and confidant tried to bring up the idea to the market but the product barely gave any fruits. It caused them a very huge loss and discouragement. Nevertheless, Gates never stopped there. He looked beyond the failure so he kept exploring new opportunities in life. Later on, his first Microsoft product opened a new path to his success.

The languish, agony and calamities are a fountain of stamina and audacity which leads us to

Page | 190

eminence. Such arduousness should be regarded as stepping stones to our destiny. Through this we learn to accept all languish believing that everything is happening for a better tomorrow.

This attitude towards languish and agony will surely harden you making you strong and it prepares you to grab that long waited achievement. Hardships are certainly a blessing in disguise. They enable you to withstand all pains with a strong heart. This moves your stagnant courage to action and you start to do great things.

Never blame your situation at all. You learn a lot during your hardships, but most importantly, take it as God's plan and a privilege that you have found a fortuity to show your brainy against languish and to come out victorious of all edges.

"Gold and silver are tested by fire" PROVERBS 17:3

So are we to have that glittering end that everybody else desires we have to go through tribulations which shapes us from all sides and brings about the best out of us. Changing your perspective is one way of appreciating adversity hence using it as an opportunity towards your goals and success. Below are some of the things you should do which can guide you through your adjustment:

1. Redefine Failure

"Failure is the greatest opportunity I have to know who I am"   -JOHN KILLINGER.

Many people take failure as a defeat, a doomed future and as the end of the world. But not unless you fail you will not have the reason to wake up and prove to the world that you are alive.

"There is no doubt in my mind that there are many ways of being a winner. But there is really only one way to be a loser. And that is to fall and not to look beyond the failure"

-KYLE ROTE JR.

Thus, when you fall down, don't accept to stay on the ground. Wake up and get moving. Focus beyond your failure. Let that be your catalyst to move on and achieve what you were destined to achieve.

2. Accept your mistakes

"By seeking and blundering we learn"
-JOHAN WOLFANG VON GOETHE

Mistakes are of course very important parts of our lives. We learn through our mistakes, we realize the reality through our mistakes, we take a turning point through the realization of our mistakes, we achieve certain goals as a result of our mistakes but most importantly, we take the right path to success due to our mistakes.

3. Win over Yourself.

"A man is not defeated by his opponent but by himself"
-JAN CHRISTIAN SMUTS

Avoid competing with others but compete with yourself. Do your best to the best of your knowledge and in the only way you know. Let your mind compete with your being. Ignore the achievements and developments of others. Just focus on yours and make sure you achieve what your heart desires. That is the best com-petition ever.

4. Ignore your past

"We are products of our past but we don't have to be prisoners of it"   *-RICK WARREN.*

Admire your past and you will always hover at the brinks of wishing. The past is already gone. It's like a dead person. The Bible states it clearly that they have no further reward.

"The dead are totally forgotten. They have no further reward." ECCLESIASTES 9:15

So is our past. It has no further reward. We must burry it and leave it behind focusing ahead. Don't let the past keep dragging you down every now and then. The past is over and completely gone. The future lies at the hands of our fucus today.

5. Be Optimistic

"A pessimist sees the difficulty in every opportunity; an optimist sees the opportunity in every difficulty."
                              -WINSTON CHURCHIL.

You must see an opportunity in each and every challenge. In a tale of sales and opportunity, two ambitious individuals were dispatched from Europe to Africa with the task of selling shoes. Upon arriving in Africa, they discovered that the local people had little to no tradition of wearing footwear. Faced with this unexpected challenge, the salespeople returned to Europe to present their findings and provide a report on their experiences. The first salesperson confidently shared their assessment, acknowledging the difficulty of selling shoes in Africa due to the prevailing lack of awareness and demand for such products. While their observation was indeed accurate, it highlighted the potential obstacles that lay ahead.

It was then the second salesperson's turn to present their report, and with a beaming smile, they embraced the opportunity before them. In response to the director's perplexed expression, the salesperson calmly explained their perspective. They acknowledged that Africans had not traditionally worn shoes, but rather than viewing this as a deterrent, they saw it as an extraordinary opportunity. The salesperson recognized the untapped market potential and envisioned themselves as a catalyst for introducing and teaching the local population about the benefits and joys of wearing shoes.

The director was captivated by the second salesperson's optimistic outlook and ability to perceive the hidden possibilities. Recognizing their visionary mindset and strategic thinking, the company appointed them as the Marketing Director for Africa, entrusted with leading a team of over 100 sales managers and agents. Meanwhile, the first salesperson, whose limited perspective had hindered their ability to see the potential, was informed that the company could not offer them a position, as their outlook did not align with the organization's entrepreneurial spirit.

This story underscores the importance of embracing challenges as opportunities for growth and innovation. The second salesperson's positive mindset, coupled with their ability to envision a market where others saw none, propelled them towards success. Their willingness to adapt, teach, and introduce a new concept in an unfamiliar environment demonstrated their entrepreneurial spirit, ultimately leading to a position of leadership and influence.

The tale serves as a reminder that in the face of adversity, it is crucial to seek out the hidden prospects that lie within challenges. By shifting our perspective and uncovering innovative solutions, we can transform obstacles into stepping stones on the path to success. The story invites us to adopt a mindset of possibility and open our eyes to the untapped potential that exists within every hurdle we encounter.

Strategic fall to fly 12

1. **Dream**

2. **Persist**

3. **Analyze your situation**

4. **Find a mentor**

5. **Brand yourself**

6. **Explore your potential**

7. **Have a vision-write down your vision**

8. **The bitter truth in action**

9. **Plan to succeed**

10. **Choose wisely**

11. **Manage your stress**

12. **Adjust your perspective**

Strategic fall to fly- The summery

Dream

Be determined more than any other time ever. Nature your relationships in all means. Be excellent in all your undertakings. Take action no matter what and finally, be a good Manager.

Persist

"I will always find a way, and a way will always find me."

-CHARLES F. GLASSM.

Quitting should never be the solution to a challenge in pursuing your goals. Remember that about 80% of people who fail, it's because they quitted before realizing their success. Always find a way and the way will always find you.

Analyse your Situation

Put your house in order. Organise everything from the outset to the end. Define
your hobbies, your interests and most importantly your aims. Give priorities as per
the needs and execute each and every plan
as soon as possible.

Find A MENTOR

A mentor is very important. At times he
will act like a catalyst to your achievements. He or she will give you sound advises and guidance.

Brand yourself

Market yourself. Do extraordinary things which will enable the world realize your greatness and existence. Be a brand of your own self.

Explore your potential

Exploring your potential simply means un-leashing your greatness. These qualities in you that are hidden and they are of the highest importance. You need to get them out of the bag and beware of the role they play once explored.

Have a vision

Bear a very clear vision and remain a visionary person. Set your goals and objectives which are the steps essential to achieve your vision. Go for them. Have a very clear picture of what you want in life. You must have the unseen site which leads you to the intended road.

Expedite

Execute your plan right away. Don't wait for tomorrow for tomorrow never comes. Avoid procrastination. This is a killer disease.

Plan to succeed

Be well focused at all time. Hang to your principles. Ignore all the other unnecessary things going around and focus on only one thing. Achieving your target.

Choose wisely

"We are our choices."
            -JEAN-PAUL SARTRE

The choices we make every day depicts who we are and where we are going to land in the near future. So be careful and choose wisely.

Manage your stress

Do not allow Stress to hover at the brinks of your mind. Clear up any mess in your mind by assuming that everything is all right. pray too.

Adjust your perspective

Change the way you view things at once. If you have been seeing the negative side of the coin all the time, this should be a turning point and start seeing positivity in everything.

***

Author's Mind

Throughout a remarkable journey spanning over 25 years, Jouvénalliss Mwendwa Kioko dedicated himself to an intense exploration of the English language and a diverse array of fields. His profound research encompassed topics ranging from leadership and responsibility to management, success and failure, politics, economics, character and behavior, love and relationships, as well as reasoning and thinking. Immersed in this rich and transformative experience, Jouvénalliss Mwendwa Kioko emerged with a profound understanding of life, nurturing a collection of philosophical and historical ideas that he yearns to share with the global community. These ideas, born from his deep knowledge and exploration of various facets of existence, hold the power to inspire and enlighten individuals from all walks of life.

Jouvénalliss Mwendwa Kioko's intellectual journey has bestowed upon him a unique perspective, allowing him to synthesize insights from different disciplines and distill them into a coherent set of principles that offer profound guidance and wisdom. These principles transcend boundaries and encapsulate the fundamental truths that underpin human existence.

With an ardent desire to contribute to the collective growth and enlightenment of humanity, Jouvénalliss Mwendwa Kioko stands ready to unveil his invaluable body of work to the world. Through his writings and teachings, he seeks to ignite a spark of inspiration, foster personal growth, and prompt meaningful introspection in individuals across the globe.

By sharing his meticulously cultivated ideas, Jouvénalliss Mwendwa Kioko aspires to uplift, transform, and empower individuals, enabling them to navigate the complexities of life with greater clarity, purpose, and fulfillment. His profound insights serve as a beacon of light, illuminating the path towards personal and societal progress. Jouvénalliss Mwendwa Kioko's unwavering dedication and passion for knowledge have led him to distill the essence of life's intricacies into a treasure trove of wisdom. Now, armed with his profound insights, he endeavors to touch the hearts and minds of people worldwide, unveiling a tapestry of profound ideas that will forever shape the way we perceive and engage with the world around us.

Relationship & behaviour

- o   Responsibility is measured by the amount of care within your inner self.

- o   Family means anyone around you. People who care about your welfare even though they might not have the capacity to improve your life vastly.

- o   The only way you can maintain your taste is by maintaining your respect.

- o   No one is perfect at all. Not even the Angeles in heaven. That's why people should learn to respect their weaknesses.

- o   Corruption is none other than twisting justice in favour of some one's favourite.

- o   The people you choose to be your friends are more likely to conform you to their own standards.

- It is not how much educated you are what matters, but how good you use the knowledge you have.
- Your real people will stick by you even when everyone else has deserted from your system.
- Respect is a two-way traffic. You give it freely you get it freely.
- Your treatment to others represents not only your inner self but also your real self.
- The only way you can punish your enemies is by doing good to them. Guiltiness and re-morse will hover at the brinks of their hearts.
- Being good is enough but being real is com-plete.
- Forgiving is the relish for being forgiven.
- The best conversion of mankind is leading by example.
- Don't invite if you are not ready to serve.

Page | 211

o   Different people can be ranked differently depending on their behaviour. Some are mannerless being a shame to their kindred while others have good manners being an epitome of perfection to the human race.

o   Yes, we are created in the image and likeness of God, but that does not mean human beings can be worshipped as some do in their positions.

o   Don't let an innocent soul be a scapegoat, you may be the next victim.

o   Don't be like the hypocrites, when they give you food, you must cook their style. When they give you money, you must spend their way. When they give you work, you must do their will and yet when you serve them, you must worship them.

o   Some one's character is the direct revelation of their capability.

- You might possess the whole world but if you lack good will, you are nothing more than a dead dog.
- The only time when bad manners is acceptable is when its consequences are being demonstrated.
- It's ironical ordering others to do what you cannot. Nothing offends more than its amplitude.
- Don't be so conceited. You have not yet reached the better half of God's creation.
- Show me a perfect person, and I will show you the source of all perfection. God Almighty.
- Goodness is like a river, when you throw dirty on it, it's easily cleaned and swept away.
- Good relationships are mentored by perfect attitudes.

- If your heart is lost you might even lose your life.

Industry and performance

- A nation without industries is like a tap without water. It looks firm and ready, but nothing to keep you busy.
- Companies which treasure the efforts of the employees usually take pleasure in its production.
- If you want to fathom a nation's ability, don't go to the treasury. Go straight to its industrial sector.
- A team player must accommodate as much as they wish to be accommodated.
- A boss is always a boss no matter how tiny and weak they are.
- A loyal servant is like justice. It never takes any law for an answer.

- There is only one boss I have known all my Life; the customer.
- Pain without gain is worthless and so is trade without profit.
- Professionalism, communication and accountability are the fundamental aspects of working smart.
- If you meet as a team, you set the base. If you walk as a team, you build the base but if you deliver as a team, you complete the circle.
- All industrialists are similar in one thing. They are economists.
- Companies which prioritise the safety of their workers, usually excel in production.
- A company's taste is maintained by the quality of its brands but not the quantity.
- Nothing matters a lot like attitude in performance. When it's excellent, the results

outstand. When it's poor, the results hit the rock bottom.

o It is a mystery to experience growth in business without experiencing a loss.

o A debt unpaid is like dirty undone. Nothing stresses more than its scathing appearance.

Life

o Knowing your fit and don't fit is the outset of a bright Destiny

o Your life is what you think of yourself.

o Never underate anyone. We are all God's work. Otherwise, you will be like a butterfly who preens its wings, yet it depends on a charity of flowers for life.

o The only way we can rate life is by the moments that take our breathes away.

o Sometimes life can be so unfair, situations are always against wishes.

o Basing on assumption, everything that we do in life is a risk including life itself.

o The price of life is always at the end of a journey but not at the beginning.

o Life is like a book. Each chapter you accomplish builds your passion to get to the next one.

o Decide on what you want in life and take action. Otherwise, you will hover at the brinks of wishing.

o Everyone in the human race possess what it takes to prosper. But it takes extraordinary efforts to get there.

o If you want your life, you must lose it at the beginning. If you lose it at the end, you might lose it for good.

o The hardest part of life connotes the finest path to your desired destiny.

- Life isn't a plate of food which you hold and the next minute you are in the process of losing and gaining. Giving and receiving. Planning and executing.
- It doesn't matter how long or short we exist on earth what matters is how we live our lives.
- It's luck for all of us who were born, but it's not luck that we will die.
- The only great reward You can achieve by serving the devil is eternal darkness. By serving God you achieve eternal glory.

Love

- Love is the epitome of gain. Hate is the hallmark of losing.
- People may distract your words, disapprove your requests, and even reject your

face. But your love alone is enough to rivet the whole world.

o   All folks huge and tiny, Rich and poor, have qualities to be loved even though they might be hidden.

o   Love is never lost. If not reciprocated, it flows back to soften and purify the heart.

o   If you want to prove your love, you must prove your trust

o   All humanity is kindred in one way or another. After all we all came from a common couple.

o   Those who love will be rewarded with love

o   Belonging is the price of love.

o   The more you love, the more you grow in feeling and affection.

Success and failure

- If you exceed your grasp, you have no further limit to success.

- While a goal is a dream with a deadline, it's also an essential step necessary to achieving your vision

- We would not have great achievements if we didn't have small attempts first.

- Your dreams and plans are of no value. They are pointless unless they are accompanied by commitment. Action is the key.

- At the beginning of every journey there is always a pall of unfathomable ordeals. You only need to be strong and firm.

- Never call success luck, people may not realize your efforts.

- A vision Is worthy equal the efforts needed to achieve it.

- People who believe in the road they have chosen, are more likely to get to their desired destination.

- Never let a fall keep you from climbing. But resist and hung to your efforts until the going gets better.

- No matters how much fear they have on failing, winners never allow fear to control them.

- It's extremely hard to determine the distance between heaven and earth. And so is to succeed without failing.

- If our plans misfire, we must not live a spell of endless blame and accept the reality which has just taken place.

- The difference between success and failure lies in the difference of their habits.

- You may fail a million times, yet success awaits you in the next trial.

- I have never seen failure, but I know people fail by impressing others.
- Trouble is an incentive to creativity
- Failing is not an issue, the issue is accepting to remain at the rock-bottom
- Success is not gained by richness, but by achieving your heart's desire and winning the affection of many.
- Laziness is a professional destructor while hard work is a professional constructor.
- Success is like children. They never hold grudges no matter how hard you hit them.
- It doesn't matter how much time you fail, what matters is how many times you get up and keep going.
- Failure is not the payment of hard work. Never. Not at all.
- Success is simply a journey unencumbered with unnecessary knowledge, and the handicap of meaningless experience.

- While success is an individual's state of mind, failure is a man's inability to reach his goals in life.
- The road to success is always rough, scathing and savoury. To travel on it you must be true and real.
- As long as your determination is superfluous, failure can never be your destiny.
- To achieve success, energy, skills and knowledge in their fullest can be good catalysts.
- Sometimes it takes extreme difficulties in the beginning to have a bright shining end.
- Darkness shows you light. While the light shows you the way.
- A single word delivered in excellence can grant you great riches and ample wealth.
- Fear is a very reliable source to failure, and indeed the first step to hell.

o Never worry because you have problems but rather worry because you don't know how to deal with the problems.

o It doesn't matter what you are passing through what matters is whether you are ready to focus beyond the trouble.

o The process of success comes through a process of Failure and constant languish.

o Failure is not as worse as many thinks. It is in fact the most crucial key that opens the firm gate of prosperity and success.

o Success is good. But it is the Greatest degree of failure if achieved through a shortcut.

o Failing to learn from your failure, is failing to achieve success.

o Being wealth is not being successful. Success is what you do with your wealth.

o   In failure you learn more than enough les-
    sons, but you might never learn a single
    lesson in success.

Safety and Health

o   Just as faith is necessary in all situations,
    safety is paramount in any working envi-
    ronment.

o   It comes a time when people have to dine
    and wine what they refer as poison so as to
    keep their health.

o   The only formula to a better health is to be
    a slave to your eating habit.

o   A change of thoughts, a change of food, a
    change in living conditions and yet a
    change of behaviour defines good health.

o   If you take a lot of time thinking of your
    good health even the bad one will vanish.

o A healthy heart is a great symbol of a wealth community.

o Health is happiness and happiness is a choice.

o You don't need a doctor to have good health but you might need one to examine your health.

o Safety begins with oneself. The more secure you are, the more likely you are to help others to be safe.

o If you lose your wealth, you can easily revamp it back, but if you lose your health., you lose your life as well.

o It is pointless to compromise with your safety hoping that things will improve. The sooner you act the better. Life is irreplaceable.

o Safety is not just being far from danger, but also a state of complacency.

o   Good health is not measured by the number of doctors you have, but by the number of smiles you manage in a normal day.

General facts

o   When support is attached to some conditions, it becomes tyranny.

o   To build a castle for the king, you must first have a hurt of your own.

o   Don't relinquish your plan simply because of a high degree of resistance. You are already on the right path.

o   While a budget directs you on what to purchase, the concept can only be determined by the size of your Wallet

o   Don't do something and regret later rather be cautious of the necessary steps to perfection.

- Several beats continuous becomes a piece of music.

- I neither support A nor Z since they are the first and the last letters in the alphabet, but I support the chronological order in which they follow.

- I may not be perfect at all, but my honesty and transparency will prove me to be a more reliable figure.

- When you do something far much beyond your capacity, you become an extraordinary figure by yourself for yourself.

- What you wish for yourself is most likely to be your end result.

- It is important. Very important to verify information from the source before exploding. Some stories are just hot wind.

- Nothing matters more than having a positive attitude. Your outlook will always influence your income.
- In the face of unbearable loss, seek comfort and solace from God
- Being a millionaire is not just having several millions in your bank account but being able to maintain the millions.
- A worthless thing always attracts many hopeless people.
- A wise person concedes correction even though it might be hurting, a fool rebel even the most Comforting advice.
- It's better to die with courage than to live with fear.
- The only way you can avoid being subject to the law is doing the will of God.
- Obedience, Honesty and truth compose the way to freedom.

- Do not put your trust in folks, they only offer a faint hope. The only real and reliable hope is celestial.

- If you boycott your responsibility now, you will have more responsibilities in the future.

- The manner you answer questions, tells more of who you are than the way you argue.

- You may recover from an illness, or injury, but you may live forever to correct a misspoken word.

- There is no miracle. I don't think there will ever be one that is greater than humanity.

- Trust is the worst of all the habits' if you trust fully, you will be deceived. If you don't trust at all, you will suffer.

- No one wants to have the future now but every one longs for it.

- It's better to be weak in the morning and be strong in the evening.
- You may be lucky to achieve a reward, but you may not be lucky to maintain it.
- If you bring up a perfect idea, you will have a million perfect opinions
- Resistance is the depiction of a reasonable decision.
- The spirit of a true warrior is to keep fighting. Perhaps losing several battles but eventually clinching the war.
- Life is all about maintaining your game. Winning where possible and loosing where necessary.

Upshot

At some point, each one of us will certainly, encounter some form of challenges and afflictions in life. It could be illness or even lack of financial stability. Again, it could be hardship in achieving your set goals and objectives. And it becomes a very big challenge to deal and conquer such situations on your path to eminence. Nevertheless, with the right mental outlook and ace in hole, conquering affliction can be easy than you may think.

- Always bear an affirmative mindset. This will help you in finding the best solution for you to get moving.
- Device a strategy of expedition by identifying the resources surrounding you and set a good plan to handle the challenge. The strategy has to be a matter of fact.

- Notably, Adversity and downfalls are part and parcel of the blazing process. In such situations, one will be able to build character Development and resilience. In most cases, many people succeed when they are faced with adversity.

- Lastly, you will find that some of the situations are within your command or mastery. Focus on this first.

ABOUT THE AUTHOR

Jouvenalliss Mwendwa Kioko is a remarkable individual who embodies the qualities of a man of God, life coach, mentor, and writer. Renowned for his training expertise and extensive global travels, he has dedicated his life to researching and imparting wisdom on various aspects of life. With a broad range of experience spanning fields such as insurance, sales and marketing, hospitality, telecommunications, manufacturing, and oil and gas, Jouvenalliss has made an impact both locally and internationally. As an accomplished author, he has penned several insightful books, including **"The Scar of Destiny," "English speaking & writing," "Resources & Mechanics of Marriage," "Oomph bells" "Boulevard of Success,"   "Spry Detective," "The Mock Pal," and "Jezebel,"** with many more upcoming works in the pipeline. His written works delve into diverse subjects, touching on personal growth, relationships, success, and overcoming adversity. Jouvenalliss' journey to success is a testament to his unwavering determination and faith in God. Born in the slums of Kibra, Nairobi, Kenya, he grew up in various estates in Nairobi, including Dandora, Mathare, Zimmerman, Githurai, Embakasi, and Pipeline. Despite facing significant challenges, he refused to let adversity define him and never gave up on his goals and dreams. Through prayer and unwavering faith, he found the strength to persevere. At the heart of Jouvenalliss' endeavors lies his vision of helping others grow. He has become an emblem of eminence and persistence through his unique approach to tackling challenges. Whenever he faced moments of doubt or the temptation to quit, he would draw upon his grand vision and rise above the immediate obstacles. His unwavering focus and determination have propelled him forward, inspiring those around him to pursue their own aspirations.

As the founder, Crew Party Chief, and CEO of Apton Crew International Ltd (ACIL), Jouvenalliss continues to make a significant impact. Additionally, he holds a graduate certificate in TESOL from the university of Birmingham, United Kingdom and is a graduate of the Holstein Training and Technologies Institute as a Safety Analyst. In his personal life, Jouvenalliss is happily married to Zemenay Mwendwa, and together they are proud parents to their children, Brummelhuis and Beelbright. His commitment to his family and his passion for uplifting others exemplify his character and values. Jouvenalliss Mwendwa Kioko stands as a beacon of hope, resilience, and unwavering determination. Through his multifaceted roles as a man of God, life coach, mentor, and writer, he continues to inspire individuals from all walks of life to overcome adversity and achieve greatness.